A Teaching Assistant's Complete Guide to Achieving NVQ Level 2

Are you a teaching assistant?
Are you enrolled or thinking of enrolling on an NVQ training course?
Or are you a tutor or assessor on such a course?

Then *A Teaching Assistant's Complete Guide to Achieving NVQ Level 2* is the book you cannot afford to be without . . .

A key element of your NVQ Teaching Assistant course is that you have to show *evidence* that you can apply your knowledge to everyday classroom activities, and students often find this is their biggest challenge. This book provides a range of tried-and-tested materials and practical advice on how to gather evidence that covers key performance indicators, to ensure that you complete your course successfully. The essential course companion will:

- Give detailed guidance on how to collect evidence to match performance indicators from a variety of sources
- Provide photocopiable resources to include templates for personal accounts, appraisals and self-appraisals
- Give examples of IEPs, Behaviour Plans and teaching planning sheets
- Provide the necessary underpinning knowledge
- Provide summaries of relevant legislation that TAs need to know
- Detail how the knowledge outlined in the text can be mapped onto the mandatory units for VQs in Support Work in Schools (SWiS) Level 2

Highly practical, rooted in everyday classroom practice and very closely tied to NVQ course requirements, this reader-friendly book will be an essential comprehensive guide for all students, as well as tutors, assessors and teachers supporting candidates for this course.

Susan Bentham is County Curriculum Co-ordinator for Vocational Pathways for West Sussex Adult Education and a lecturer at the University of Chichester, UK.

Roger Hutchins is the Inclusion Manager at two primary schools in Portsmouth, UK.

A Teaching Assistant's Complete Guide to Achieving NVQ Level 2

How to meet your performance indicators

Susan Bentham and
Roger Hutchins

LONDON AND NEW YORK

First published 2007
by Routledge
2 Park Square, Milton Park, Abingdon, Oxon OX14 4RN

Simultaneously published in the USA and Canada
by Routledge
270 Madison Ave, New York, NY 10016

Routledge is an imprint of the Taylor & Francis Group, an informa business

Typeset in Sabon and Gill Sans by
Florence Production Ltd, Stoodleigh, Devon
Printed and bound in Great Britain by
The Cromwell Press, Trowbridge, Wiltshire

British Library Cataloguing in Publication Data
A catalogue record for this book is available from the British Library

Library of Congress Cataloging in Publication Data
A catalog record for this book has been requested

ISBN10: 0–415–40341–3 (pbk)
ISBN10: 0–203–96484–5 (ebk)

ISBN13: 978–0–415–40341–2 (pbk)
ISBN13: 978–0–203–96484–2 (ebk)

Contents

Figures

Acknowledgements

Susan Bentham says: Thanks to my family, colleagues, especially Karen, Jackie and Terry and my many students for their support and a very special thank you to my son, Matthew – for his great artwork!

Roger Hutchins says 'Thank you' to Anne and to the staff at both schools for their continuing support, hard work and dedication.

Glossary

Active listening Communicating to the person we are talking with that we have indeed heard and understood them, accomplished by techniques such as rewording and reflecting.

Annual reviews Legal reviews to be held at least once a year for pupils who have a statement of special educational need.

Assessment (formative) Ongoing, continuous assessment which measures progress in small stages and informs planning for future teaching.

Assessment (summative) Formal testing which assesses how much pupils have learnt in a particular subject or over a specific time period.

Assessment for Learning Assessing and marking children's work in a way which sets them targets.

Attainment levels/targets – see National Curriculum

Attention Deficit/Hyperactivity Disorder (ADD/ADHD) Medical diagnoses which describe a range of emotional and/or behavioural difficulties such as extreme impulsivity, inattentiveness and continuous activity (always on the go). Evident before the age of 7 and constant in different contexts.

Auditory learners – see Learning styles

Autism/Autistic Spectrum Disorder (ASD) Severely impairs a person's ability to maintain normal contact with the world. Appears before the age of 3.

Board of Governors Those with the legal responsibility of ensuring that the school is following correct national and local procedures. They are volunteers drawn from a range of places who act as 'critical friends' to schools.

Child Protection Liaison Officer (CPLO) The designated member of staff who is responsible for overseeing and administering issues relating to child protection.

Children Looked After (CLA) All children and young people who are on Care Orders or who are accommodated under the Children Act 1989 or who are remanded into the care of the local authority.

Common Assessment Framework (CAF) Arising from *Every Child Matters*, the CAF enables every agency working with children in England to use the same initial assessment to identify needs or potential need in children from conception to age 19. The terminology used and the process engaged in will be common to all agencies, thus promoting 'joined-up information sharing and responses'. As a result of the CAF, a 'Lead Professional' will be identified who will liaise with all agencies involved and will be the single point of contact with the family.

Differentiation A means by which teachers offer a common curriculum to all pupils in their classes, but tailored to meet the needs of individuals.

Dyslexia Primarily a specific difficulty with learning to read, write and/or spell, often accompanied by poor organisational skills.

Dyspraxia (Developmental Coordination Disorder) Impairment of the organisation of movement that is often accompanied by problems with language, perception and thought. Handwriting is often a particular difficulty, along with clumsiness. Symptoms are evident from an early age, often from birth.

Educational Psychologists (EPs) Qualified teachers who have trained further in psychology. Support pupils and adults working with pupils who are experiencing sustained difficulties in learning or behaviour. Not to be confused with medical psychiatrists.

Education Welfare Service (EWS) Local authority staff working with students and families who have social difficulties with school such as poor attendance.

Ethnic minority Any pupil who is identified by parents/carers as belonging to any ethnic group other than 'white British'. NB Parents/carers have the right not to state an ethnic identity.

Foundation Stage Pre-National Curriculum schooling curriculum – followed in Reception and Early Years of infant or primary schools.

Gifted and talented Those pupils identified in school as being the most able in academic subjects or the most talented in areas such as art, sport or music.

Higher Level Teaching Assistant (HLTA) A status given to TAs who reach certain standards of education and performance which enables them to be given greater spheres of responsibility in schools.

Ideal self How an individual would like to be.

Inclusion The process whereby, so far as possible and in compliance with parental preference, all pupils regardless of ability or disability are educated in their local mainstream schools.

Individual Behaviour Plan (IBP) A tool to plan intervention to modify pupil behaviour – sets out what is expected from the pupil and states how the school and home will support the pupil in reaching these targets.

Individual Education Plan (IEP) A tool to plan intervention for pupils with special educational needs – sets out what should be taught which is *additional to* or *different from* what would normally be delivered in the class, focusing on three or four short-term targets which are SMART (specific, measurable, attainable, relevant and timed).

Interactive whiteboard An ICT tool linked to the teacher's personal computer or laptop which enables programs to be displayed in front of the whole class and which enables pupils and teachers to write their own comments and notations.

Kinaesthetic learners – see **Learning styles**

Learning objectives The focus of any one particular lesson which should be understood by all pupils and their work assessed in relation to that learning objective.

Learning styles An individual's unconscious preference in regard to how they process and learn new information. Some learn better through hearing (**auditory learners**), others through what they see (**visual learners**) and others through what they touch or handle (**kinaesthetic learners**). Most employ a combination of all three learning styles which is why schools seek to teach using 'VAK' techniques (visual, auditory and kinaesthetic).

Local authority The body comprised of elected members (councillors) and employed officers who, together, are responsible for a range of services in a given local area, including all services for children. There are one hundred and fifty local authorities in England and Wales.

Multiple intelligences The view that children and adults are skilled and able in a wider range of activities than 'reading, writing and arithmetic'.

Multi-sensory Materials which seek to employ as many senses as possible in the learning process.

National Curriculum The National Curriculum sets out the minimum that has to be taught in schools, and a framework against which attainment can be measured. For each subject there are *programmes of study* which set out what pupils should be taught, and *attainment targets* which set the level of performance pupils are expected to achieve.

National Literacy Strategy (NLS) Introduced in 1998 to provide teaching plans for literacy to put the National Curriculum into practice in primary schools, it gives teaching objectives for each term.

National Numeracy Strategy (NNS) Introduced in 1999, it illustrates how maths can be taught from Reception to Year 6. 'Key objectives' are set out for each year group. The NNS established a daily 'numeracy hour', with an emphasis on mental maths and a variety of teaching and recording strategies.

Pastoral Support Plan (PSP) This is similar to an Individual Behaviour Plan but is more detailed and is put into place when a pupil is at risk of being excluded from school.

Personal Education Plan (PEP) Plan drawn up by social services in conjunction with other services such as education for a child who is being looked after by the local authority.

Phonics The 'building blocks' of written language allowing the 'decoding' of written words into sounds or the construction of written sounds into words.

Phonological awareness/phonology Awareness of sounds within words – e.g. ability to generate rhyme and alliteration, or to segment and blend sounds.

Programmes of study – see **National Curriculum**

Provision map A means of outlining what is being provided for pupils in addition to or different from what is normally provided in class. It shows what is being provided, who it is being provided for and what the aim of that provision is. Over time it states the value of that provision by measuring progress gained and relating this with the cost of providing that extra support.

QCAs National tests published by the Qualification and Curriculum Authority (QCA) used voluntarily by schools at the end of Years 3, 4 and 5.

Scheme of work What schools decide to teach in a particular subject or topic taken from the National Curriculum within a limited time frame (e.g. one term).

Self-image How an individual describes themselves.

Social learning theory This theory states that children learn by watching and imitating others.

Special educational needs (SEN) '*A child has special educational needs if he or she has a learning difficulty which may be the result of a physical or sensory disability, an emotional or behavioural problem or developmental delay*' (Education Act

1981). 'Children have special educational needs if they have a *learning difficulty* which calls for *special educational provision* to be made for them' (Education Act 1996, Section 312).

Special Educational Needs Coordinator (SENCO) The person or persons in school responsible for overseeing the day-to-day operation of special needs provision.

Specialist Teacher Adviser Teachers employed by the local authority who specialise in certain subjects such as hearing impairment or visual impairment. Their role is to support schools by giving advice about specific pupils.

Speech and Language Therapists Health professionals who assess and review individual children, provide resources and give advice where there is a concern over language.

Standard Attainment Tasks (SATs) National tests published by QCA which schools must use at the end of Key Stages 1, 2 and 3 to measure pupil progress and the effectiveness of teaching.

Statements of Special Educational Need Documents regulated by law setting out the educational and non-educational needs of individuals and the provision to be put in place to meet those needs.

Teaching styles The way in which an individual approaches the teaching process. Teaching style includes aspects of student involvement and emphasis on the importance of rules. Often an individual's teaching style is based on their preferred learning styles and their experience of teaching.

Visual learners – see Learning styles

Chapter 1

Overview of NVQ course – what you need to know before you begin

Getting started

Congratulations! Starting a National Vocational Qualification (NVQ) course for teaching assistants is both challenging and exciting. NVQs for teaching assistants (TAs) are based on the National Occupational Standards produced by the Local Government National Training Organisation (LGNTO 2001). NVQs are designed to provide valid and relevant vocational qualifications that are valued by the workforce. Gaining an NVQ can provide progression routes to further training and career opportunities. Those who complete an NVQ Level 2 may wish to continue on to an NVQ Level 3. Those who gain an NVQ 3 may wish to apply for the Higher Level Teaching Assistant (HLTA) award or possibly enrol on a foundation degree. And of course a foundation degree can be the first step towards a teaching qualification. However, whatever level you are at and whatever level you wish to aspire to, enrolling on an NVQ course will give you the opportunity to study and discover more about supporting the students you are working with. An NVQ gives you the opportunity to reflect or think about what you are doing in the classroom and to think about how you can improve on your practice.

NVQs for teaching assistants are worthwhile but they are also hard work. This book aims to help you through that process.

One of the first questions TAs enrolling on an NVQ course ask is what does an NVQ involve? What do I have to do?

NVQs are about demonstrating that you are competent at a particular task or skill, for example being able to give feedback to the teacher on the pupil's response to a certain activity. **Competence** is about demonstrating that you are able to do a task and demonstrating that you understand why that task is important.

Therefore an NVQ requires you to:

- Show that you are able to do the task. This requires you to provide evidence of **performance.**
- Show that you understand why that task is important. This requires you to provide evidence of underpinning **knowledge.**

To complete an NVQ you will need to provide evidence of **performance and knowledge.** Let's go back to our example of giving feedback to the teacher regarding pupils' responses to a certain activity.

In regard to providing evidence of **performance** you will need to give examples of occasions when you have provided the teacher with feedback.

In regard to providing evidence of **knowledge** you will need to show that you understand why it is important to give feedback in a constructive manner and how feedback relates to the planning and evaluation of learning activities.

Structure of the course

The NVQ 2 Teaching Assistants course is divided into units of competence. To achieve the NVQ 2 a teaching assistant needs to complete seven units of competence.

There are four **mandatory units** of competence. You must complete these units.

Unit 2.1 Help with classroom resources and records.
Unit 2.2 Help with the care and support of pupils.
Unit 2.3 Provide support for learning activities.
Unit 2.4 Provide effective support for your colleagues.

There are five **optional units**. For the NVQ 2 course you will need to complete three.

The optional units are:

Unit 2.5 Support literacy and numeracy activities in the classroom.
Unit 3.1 Contribute to the management of pupil behaviour.
Unit 3.10 Support the maintenance of pupil safety and security.
Unit 3.11 Contribute to the health and well-being of pupils.
Unit 3.17 Support the use of information and communication technology (ICT) in the classroom.

Which units you choose to complete very much depends on your role within the school. For example, a teaching assistant supporting pupils in Reception and Year 1 might choose to select:

- Support literacy and numeracy (as this is what the TA does every day).
- Contribute to the health and well-being of pupils.
- Support the use of information and communication technology (as perhaps the TA has been given special responsibility for working with ICT and is recently undergoing training in interactive whiteboards).

However, another TA working for the science department in a secondary school might choose the options of:

- Contribute to the management of pupil behaviour.
- Support the maintenance of pupil safety and security (this unit being especially relevant to health and safety work within a science lab).
- Support the use of ICT in the classroom.

So we see that what you choose to cover for an optional unit really depends on what you do on a day-to-day level.

Let's get complicated

Once you have settled on what units you are going to cover, you will need to start the lengthy process of collecting evidence. Each unit is subdivided into elements or smaller units and each of these requires you to demonstrate evidence regarding both performance and knowledge.

Individuals who choose to do this course are often referred to as candidates. Teaching assistants who enrol on this course will come from a variety of backgrounds. Teaching assistants could be working in primary, secondary or special schools. Some TAs will be in paid employment while some will be working in a volunteer capacity. TAs come in all shapes and sizes (see Figure 1.1).

Some TAs who enrol on this course will do so through colleges while others might be working towards the qualification within their school as a form of in-house training. Regardless of how you are doing the course, all candidates will have an assessor. An assessor will guide candidates through the process, help them collect the required evidence and give feedback on evidence.

Once you have enrolled on this course you will receive a copy of all the standards, that is performance indicators and knowledge base criteria that you will need to provide evidence for. Do not panic. Your assessor is there to guide you.

What is evidence?

In NVQ speak, for evidence to be accepted as evidence it needs to be valid, reliable, sufficient, authentic and current.

Figure 1.1 TAs come in all shapes and sizes

Valid

To be valid, the way in which assessment is carried out and the nature of the evidence collected must be appropriate, that is, it really must demonstrate the competence of a candidate. For example, to demonstrate competence in giving teachers feedback on pupil performance, it is not enough for the candidate to write a statement saying that they do this on a day-to-day basis. The candidate will need to present evidence in regard to how they do this, for example the candidate may

- include reading and spelling records that they have filled in
- have the teacher write a statement regarding how they report on pupil performance
- write a personal account of how they give feedback, which is countersigned by the teacher.

Reliable

Reliability refers to consistency. Here reliable can be interpreted in several ways. On the one hand, does the candidate provide evidence of performing this behaviour on more than one occasion and in a variety of situations? On the other hand, reliability refers to consistency between assessors. If the evidence is reliable then all assessors should judge it as valid evidence.

Sufficient

Sufficient means that the evidence presented by the candidate is enough to prove competence. If the evidence is not sufficient it may mean that the candidate needs to write or say more. For example, a photocopy of the school's Behaviour Policy is not sufficient evidence that the candidate understands the school's Behaviour Policy. A candidate may be required to write a short summary of the Behaviour Policy focusing on their role and others' roles within this policy. A candidate may be questioned by an assessor on their understanding of the Behaviour Policy.

Authentic

This relates to whether the evidence produced is genuine and has been produced by the candidate. It is important that all personal accounts are countersigned by a witness to say that this event did happen as described. It is important that the witness is familiar with and knowledgeable of the standards relating to the work of teaching assistants. For example, a teaching assistant in showing that they complete records relating to the availability and supply of classroom resources might include a copy of a memo that they sent to the teacher stating that there were shortages of paper. For the memo to be regarded as authentic evidence, the memo will need to be countersigned by the person who received it.

Current

The evidence produced must reflect current understanding and practices.

All evidence that is presented must be valid, reliable, sufficient, authentic and current to count as appropriate evidence. All the above points may seem complicated but they are essential to ensure the integrity and quality of the qualification. When you present your evidence, an assessor will be judging your evidence on the above points and give you any necessary advice.

Ways of gathering evidence

Personal accounts

A personal account can be compared to a diary in which you describe 'what you did' during a particular period of time at school. What you write, in the personal account, will need to be matched to performance indicators. Personal accounts, in order to be considered as appropriate and authentic, will need to be countersigned by someone who has observed what you have done, usually this will be the teacher.

There is a real art to writing personal accounts. Many examples of different ways of writing personal accounts will be given in this book. Templates for writing various forms of personal accounts can be found in the appendix. In addition to help you get started, a 'writing personal accounts and matching exercise' can be found on page 221.

Case studies

A case study involves a short account of one individual student and your interaction with them. Again the case study will need to be signed by a witness to ensure that it is genuine.

Products of performance

These will often support your personal accounts. These could be individual or session plans, feedback forms, reading records or copies of **Individual Educational Plans** (**IEPs**). Confidentiality is important. It is essential that when writing personal accounts or case studies that you do not use the full names of pupils who you are working with. Some candidates refer to the pupils by their initials. If including copies of IEPs as supporting evidence, it is important to block out names.

Witness testimony

Colleagues in the workplace can write a short statement describing your practice. Their statement can provide evidence of your performance. Again, witnesses need to be familiar with the work of teaching assistants. Your assessor will give you more details in regard to who can be a witness and the relevant forms that witnesses will need to sign.

Observation

Direct assessment in the workplace can be carried out by a classroom teacher, **Higher Level Teaching Assistant (HLTA)**, **Special Educational Needs Coordinator (SENCO)** or college assessor. These individuals will write up their observations and these observations can be used as evidence.

Questioning

Your assessor may ask for more details regarding what they have observed, what you have written in a personal account or on issues relating to underpinning knowledge.

Professional discussion

This will involve having a discussion with your assessor on aspects of your role. This conversation will be taped and used as evidence. A professional discussion is more than just answering a set of questions as it allows the candidate to demonstrate their understanding of their role.

Accreditation of prior learning

Your past experience relating to courses attended, qualifications gained may provide evidence. You will need to talk to your assessor regarding this as evidence, to be considered valid, will need to be judged as current, that is, reflecting up-to-date understanding and practices.

Written knowledge

Certain elements require you to demonstrate knowledge and understanding, this can be shown by writing answers to various questions.

What you need to do

As a candidate enrolling on an NVQ 2 course for teaching assistants your responsibilities are to

- identify and collect evidence to meet the required indicators for knowledge and performance
- present the evidence in a structured format called a portfolio.

This might seem overwhelming to begin with but there are many people who will help you in this process (see Figure 1.2).

Who will help you

The course tutor

If you enrol for a course run through a college the course tutor will be responsible in part for delivering the course. They will give you valuable advice regarding how to collect evidence and set up your portfolio as well as discussing issues relating to underpinning knowledge.

The assessor

The role of an assessor is to look at the evidence you present and to make judgements regarding whether the evidence meets the required indicators or not. They are there to help you collect the necessary evidence.

Figure 1.2 Where to start?

The mentor

Candidates may have a special person within the school to whom they can go and ask for help and advice.

Internal verifier

An internal verifier may be based in a college. They are responsible for ensuring that the quality and the integrity of the course is maintained. In particular they need to ensure that all assessors are marking to the same standard.

External verifier

All NVQ 2 courses for teaching assistants are accredited through exam boards. An external verifier is employed by the exam board to visit various colleges and centres who are offering the course to ensure that all centres are maintaining the appropriate standards.

How this book will help you

This book aims to help you complete the process of an NVQ by

- providing you with examples of how to collect the required evidence through personal accounts, case studies and products of performance
- covering relevant underpinning knowledge

- giving examples of how to use feedback from assessors to improve your work
- providing photocopiable resources – for example, templates for personal accounts (see pages 200–220)
- outlining summaries of important government documents plus website references (see Chapters 12 and 13)
- presenting a Glossary of important terms (see pages ix–xii). The first time a word from the Glossary appears in the text it will in bold.

Who are Miranda, Nicola, Nazreen and friends?

One request often heard by candidates just starting an NVQ 2 is to have a look at someone else's completed portfolio – just to get an idea about what is expected. In this book we have presented examples of ongoing work submitted by three imaginary candidates. Miranda works in a primary school, Nicola works in a secondary school and Nazreen works in a junior school. In a sense this book tells the story of their struggles to put forward a portfolio of evidence. As you will see some of their evidence is better presented than others. At all points both their teacher and assessor will give comments about their work. The assessor will explain terminology and give ideas about how to collect further evidence. It is hoped that through this ongoing dialogue between the assessor and the candidates you will acquire a real sense of what is needed to gain this qualification.

Confidentiality is important. At some points first names may be used in writing personal accounts and at other points initials may be used. When you start to write your personal accounts, check with your assessor to agree procedures regarding confidentiality.

All names of characters used in this book are fictitious and any relationship to any real person or persons is purely coincidental.

Advice on starting out from an assessor

- Get organised!
- Some candidates find it easier to separate evidence for *Knowledge Base* and *Performance Indicator standards* into separate binders.
- Use your time wisely.

Tips on writing personal accounts

- It is always helpful to read the standards (indicators that you are required to cover) carefully before beginning to write a personal account. If you have already provided several pieces of evidence for a standard it isn't worth your time writing up another personal account showing that you have met the standard again!
- Use appropriate terminology to enable you to match the standard. Sometimes you can incorporate the words from the standard into what you write.
- Do not waffle. Keep the personal account concise and to the point.
- Always look out for opportunities to cross-reference your evidence to other units. This will cut down on the work you have to do.

- Remember it is not necessary to provide a personal account for every single performance indicator. It is better practice to collect evidence from a variety of sources. For example:
  - copies of students' work
  - copies of memos you have written
  - copies of reading records/student records
  - photographic evidence
  - a record of a conversation you may have had, however brief, with a member of staff regarding a student
  - a note received from a parent or guardian
  - copies of differentiated work you have provided
  - minutes of meetings you have attended.

All these sources of evidence will need to be **annotated**. Annotation requires that you write a few lines explaining what the evidence means and how it meets the standard.

Also you must maintain confidentiality at all times. Names of students should be removed from documents before placing them in your portfolio.

Finally, have fun!

Chapter 2

Unit 2.1 Help with classroom resources and records

In this unit there are two elements:

2.1.1 Help with the organisation of the learning environment
2.1.2 Help with classroom records

KNOWLEDGE BASE

2.1.1 Help with the organisation of the learning environment

Checking the availability of safety equipment

Every school has a duty of care to its pupils. This means that the teaching assistant's first responsibility, as that of all staff, is to ensure the safety and health of the children. It is important, therefore, for teaching assistants to become familiar with all aspects of health and safety – school policy, the staff who are trained First Aiders, who the school's Health and Safety Representative is, and where all relevant equipment can be found.

You need to know what to do and who to turn to in the event of an accident or a child becoming ill. You need to be aware of the children who have allergies or chronic illnesses. There should be medical protocols for any such pupils clearly visible at least in the staff room and the school office which outline procedures which must be followed in the event of an incident.

The learning environment

The learning environment is more than the classroom. During their careers, primary school TAs are likely to work with children in areas given over to cooking, science, design and technology, ICT, physical education (PE) and possibly art or music. These could be separate rooms or simply designated areas in the school. In secondary schools each room is likely to be given over to a specialist subject. The TA needs to be familiar with where these specific areas are located and with the routines associated with each area.

Schools will have areas allocated to storing resources for particular activities. It is worth investigating these. Any TA will say that one of the most frustrating things about school is not being able to find what you are looking for when you want it, or, when you do locate it, to find out that bits are missing, batteries not charged or whatever, which renders the equipment useless. It is important, therefore, to minimise stress by making yourself as familiar as you can with where things are kept throughout the school. This includes how they are stored, who monitors what is taken out, how their removal or use is recorded and who oversees their return.

Personnel responsibilities

Each school will have specific staff with responsibilities for various aspects of the learning environment. You need to know who these people are so that you can go to the appropriate person for advice or help. If a piece of ICT equipment fails, for instance, you will need to know the procedure for reporting it.

School caretaker

Often working 'behind the scenes', school caretakers are responsible for maintaining the safety of the physical learning environment of the school. They carry out repairs such as changing light bulbs or mending chairs and oversee more major maintenance issues. Teaching assistants should know the procedures in their schools for reporting maintenance issues.

Health and Safety Representative

There will be one member of staff who is the Health and Safety Representative. Their responsibility is to work alongside the caretaker to ensure the school environment is both healthy and safe. They make regular reports to the school's **Board of Governors** regarding safety aspects of the school.

Governing body

Legally, the governors of a school are responsible for the safety of the learning environment. Their responsibility is to ensure that all aspects of health and safety legislation are being met by the school. They will conduct regular inspections of the school to monitor the state of the buildings and grounds.

Subject managers

These are members of the teaching staff who have specific responsibilities for different subjects which range from coordinating the planning and delivery of those subjects across the school to ensuring that adequate resources are both available and are working for their subject area.

Ordering stock

Usually stock is ordered via the school office. As a TA you will need to know the particular procedures used in your school for ordering stock. You need to know how you should report shortages of materials such as pencils or pens.

Inclusive education

Inclusion

One of the main driving forces behind education currently, both nationally and internationally, is the principle of **inclusion**. Essentially this means that every pupil, no matter what their need, has the right to be educated in their local mainstream school. While it is usually acknowledged that there will always be pupils for whom some form of special school is needed, the underlying presumption is that all children will be educated together. The implications for mainstream schools are enormous. Rather than try to help the pupil adapt to the school (the principle of integration) the school needs to adapt to meet the needs of its pupils. This includes adapting the learning environment.

Inclusion and the learning environment

When considering the learning environment, consideration must be given to the following: lighting, noise levels and accessibility.

Lighting

All children must be able to see appropriately. Pupils with a visual impairment may require some adaptation to the lighting in the classroom or to the seating position within the class. They might need more focused, direct lighting or, alternatively, more subdued and less intense light.

Noise levels

Pupils with hearing impairments or with extra sensitivity to sound must be taken into account when the learning environment is planned and set out. So far as possible, such pupils need to be sat in quiet areas rather than close to noisy equipment or places.

Accessibility

Not every pupil with a disability is in a wheelchair – but some will be. Classrooms and specialist teaching areas, as well as the outside areas, need to be made accessible to these pupils. Some pupils may also require specialist seating which is larger than the norm and this will have an impact on the classroom.

Applying knowledge in practice

You need to show you apply this knowledge in practice. You could do this by including a case study of how you helped adjust the learning environment to ensure the inclusion of an individual or a group of pupils.

Your role and responsibility for helping to organise the learning environment

As a TA you will need to be aware of both the general needs of the pupils in the class, and the specific needs of individual pupils.

Figure 2.1 Pupils need to have chairs and desks which are appropriate to their physical size

General needs of pupils

Generally, all pupils require similar things from the learning environment – space, light, warmth, safety. They also need to have chairs and desks or tables which are appropriate to their physical size and development (see Figure 2.1). Children need to sit properly in order to write correctly – this requires them sitting with their bottoms on chairs, all four legs of the chair on the floor, the soles of their feet touching the floor and paper and pens or pencils at the correct angle. This will be different for left-handed and right-handed writers.

All pupils should be able to see the teacher or adult who is addressing the class without craning their necks. Similarly, they should be able to see any whole-class equipment, such as a whiteboard, with ease.

They should have equal access to class resources such as pencils, pens, paper, scissors – and these should be kept in safe places, such as scissor racks. Part of your responsibility is to know what resources the classroom has, where they are kept and how they are to be used. The class teacher will have instructed the children on the safe use of equipment, and your role is to reinforce such instruction.

Specific needs of individual pupils

As well as being aware of the general requirements of all pupils, you should be aware of the needs of specific individuals. The class teacher and Special Educational Needs Coordinator will have alerted you to such needs within the class, which should be written out on Individual Education Plans. These may be incorporated into a document called a **Provision Map**. You should have access to these documents as you are likely to be working with these particular pupils.

You need to be aware of any physical needs that pupils have in the class – such as a sloping board for a pupil with visual impairment. You will also need to be aware of any medical needs within the class, such as pupils with chronic illnesses like diabetes, or with severe allergies which could result in shock. You need to know where appropriate medicines are kept for such pupils and what procedures are to be followed in the event of these being needed.

Use of equipment and resources

All primary schools have a huge range of equipment in their classes – textbooks, writing materials, exercise books, paper, maths resources such as rulers, dice, clocks, number games and so on. Secondary schools will have resources appropriate to the subject areas being taught in that classroom. As a TA you need to agree with the class or subject teacher what your role and responsibility is regarding the use of this equipment.

Classroom resources fall into three categories – general classroom items, curriculum specific classroom resources and equipment, and written materials – plus specific resources.

General classroom items

General classroom items are those things used in any and every lesson and so should be available at all times – pencils, pens, rubbers, rulers, scissors, paper and the like.

Curriculum specific classroom resources and equipment

Curriculum specific items are, as the name suggests, linked to specific subjects within the curriculum and are therefore likely to be used only when those particular lessons are being taught. This includes maths equipment such as multilink, number lines, compasses, graph paper and protractors. Science equipment, specific ICT software, musical instruments and art materials will also come into this category.

Written materials

Written materials are items which are both already written (e.g. books and handouts) and which can be written upon (e.g. worksheets).

Specific resources

There will also be resources available for use in different areas of the school such as small games equipment, PE equipment such as mats and wall bars, play materials in the early years and so on.

What safety equipment is kept in different learning environments

Whenever you work with pupils, issues of health and safety should be in the forefront of your thinking. It is all too easy to assume that everything is as it should be, but constant vigilance needs to be maintained.

Along with the teacher, your role is to be on the lookout for potential hazards in the class, such as a loose electrical lead dragging across the floor or a bag left lying in front of an exit (see Figure 2.2). You should also be aware of any safety equipment within the learning environment in which you are working, such as knowing where the first aid boxes are kept. It is more likely in secondary schools that there will be specific safety

Figure 2.2 TAs need to be on the lookout for potential hazards

equipment kept in science laboratories. You need to be aware of what there is and how it should be used, in what circumstances and by whom.

The school's Health and Safety Policy

Like any public body, schools come under the legislation of the Health and Safety at Work Act 1974. This means that employers have a legal responsibility to ensure that the place of work is safe and that emergency procedures are in place and are regularly practised. There is also a legal obligation upon all employees to take care of themselves and others, to use equipment safely and in line with correct procedures, and only to use equipment they have been trained to use.

Schools must produce a Health and Safety Policy which should be regularly reviewed by staff and governors. As a TA you need to be familiar with your particular school's policy which, while being generally similar to every other such policy, will set out specific guidelines and procedures for your school. Every member of staff must by law follow the principles and procedures set out in this policy.

Checklist

- ✔ I am familiar with the health and safety policy and procedures in my school.
- ✔ I know where all the safety equipment is in the school.
- ✔ I know how to act safely in school.
- ✔ I can help organise the learning environment so all pupils are safe and have their physical needs met.

2.1.2 Help with classroom records

The record keeping systems and procedures used within the school

In one way or another, the following list of records will be kept within each school: school records, class records, individual records and teacher records. You need to find out from the appropriate people what exactly is in place in your school. Many of these records will be stored on computers.

School records

School records are usually kept in the school office. They will include the following:

- pupil name and address, parental/carer contact and emergency phone numbers
- ethnic information
- medical information
- attendance data
- accidents and injuries
- sanctions including exclusions
- rewards
- racial harassment incidents
- social services involvement including child protection issues
- school transfer
- generic behaviour records, e.g. playground incident slips
- academic records and reports from previous years.

Class records

Class records are common to the whole class, and are usually kept in the class. They will include the following:

- **formative assessment**: work completed and marked, curricula targets met, homework marked, work discussed with pupils
- **summative assessment** results: internal teacher assessment noting levels achieved and national tests (e.g. **Standard Attainment Tasks** (**SATs**))
- current school report for each child
- rewards and sanctions
- school trip information.

Individual records

Individual records are not common to the whole class, and are usually kept in class. They will include the following:

- Individual Education Plans (IEPs)
- **Individual Behaviour Plans** (**IBPs**)/**Pastoral Support Plans** (**PSPs**)
- **Personal Education Plans** (**PEPs**) for **Children Looked After** (**CLA**)
- External agency reports such as **Educational Psychologists, Speech and Language Therapists** and **Specialist Teacher Advisers**
- **Common Assessment Framework** (**CAF**).

Teacher records

Teacher records are kept in the class, and include the following:

- schemes of work
- medium and short-term planning.

Roles and responsibilities within the school for maintaining the record keeping systems

It is essential that all records are accurate and up to date:

- Medical records, such as the dosage of medicine needed to be given in the event of an emergency.
- Contact phone numbers and addresses for pupils.
- Attendance records need to be monitored on a frequent basis to ensure all pupils are attending appropriately. Where no reason is given for an absence this must be registered as an 'unauthorised absence'. Schools will keep a record of poor attendance and the involvement of the **Educational Welfare Service** may be requested.
- Records of attainment are not only for internal school use, but also sent to the **local authority**, which in turn collates information from all schools in its area and forwards these to central government.

It is obviously important, therefore, that each school has clearly defined roles and responsibilities for maintaining its records.

Normally all records kept in the school office are maintained by the administration staff. Most, if not all, will be computerised.

Class teachers have the responsibility of maintaining records kept in their classes and it is here that your role as a TA is likely to have an impact. Teachers have a responsibility not only to maintain accurate records, but also to ensure that this information is passed on to the school office, head teacher or head of year to enable whole-school analysis of data.

All staff have a duty to report accidents and record them in accordance with school policy.

Further records will be maintained by members of staff with specific responsibilities such as **special educational needs (SEN), ethnic minorities** and **gifted and talented pupils.** Some kind of whole-school register should be kept by the person(s) responsible for these areas, which is updated termly. Subject managers may also keep their own records, for instance, the music manager may keep records of which pupils are learning musical instruments in school.

You need to find out which person is responsible for which area of record keeping in your school. It may be worth completing a table such as the one shown on page 19. You can find a photocopiable blank copy in the Appendix (page 203). Some of this table has been filled in.

You need to find out what specific roles and responsibilities you have as a TA to maintain records (see Figure 2.3). It is likely, for instance, that if you are working with pupils who have **Statements of Special Educational Need** you will be required to keep

Figure 2.3 Do not let paperwork overwhelm you

records of your work with them so that you can contribute accurately to their **annual reviews**. You should view records yourself only under the direction of the teacher, SENCO or other responsible person; and, along with every other member of staff, you should never remove records from their appropriate place.

School policy for storage and security of pupil records, including confidentiality requirements

Clearly all these records are sensitive, many containing information of a confidential nature. Only those with genuine reason should have access to these records. You need to find out exactly how your school responds to this. Most schools will, however, employ similar principles:

- Whole school records and pupil files will be kept in the school office in lockable filing cabinets with the keys held only by the office staff and head teacher or member of the senior management team.
- Pupil files will not be let out of the school office so that persons viewing them can be monitored by office staff.
- All school office computers will have personal passwords which are known only to those who operate them.
- Memory discs containing information will be locked away when not in use.
- Class records will be kept safely and placed out of reach of children (in the case of primary schools).
- Individual pupil records kept by SENCOs and others with school-wide responsibilities will also be kept in a secure place – often in the school office or in lockable cabinets in those people's rooms.
- Any unwanted paper records must be disposed of appropriately – shredded if possible – to ensure that they cannot be read later.

Record keeping in the school

Member of staff	*Responsibilities for record keeping*
Administration officer	
School secretary	Keeps all medical records, parent/carer contact forms and ensures all pupil files are up to date. Uses electronic system to keep check on attendance.
Head teacher	Collates all data on academic progress of pupils, and analyses these.
Deputy head teacher	
Head of year	
Subject managers	
Classroom teachers	
SENCO	Keeps records of IEPs, reports from external agencies, records of contact with parents/carers for pupils on the SEN Register. Also keeps record of provision for SEN in the school including deployment of teaching assistants.
Ethnic minority manager	
Gifted and talented manager	
Caretaker	Records of maintenance undertaken and needed, records of fire drills and safety checks.
Others (specify)	

Whatever the case in your school, there should be clear procedures in place and you need to become aware of these.

However, it is not records who talk, it is people. All school staff must be aware of their duty of confidentiality. This means that no one, teachers or TAs, should discuss information regarding pupils with any unauthorised person. Trust takes time to build, but can be destroyed very quickly. Schools need to operate in an atmosphere where trust exists between staff and parents.

The legal implications and restrictions covering the recording and use of personal information including the Data Protection Act, the Children Act, the Freedom of Information Act and the statementing process

Data Protection Act 1998

The aim of the Data Protection Act protects the rights of the individual by ensuring that any information kept is accurate and is protected.

The Children Act 1989

This Act enshrines in law the principle that the interest of the child must always be put first.

The Children Act 2004

This Act provides the legal underpinning for the government's initiative *Every Child Matters: Change for Children.*

Freedom of Information Act 2000

Schools must produce a 'publication scheme' which sets out the type of information published by the school, how it will be published and whether or not it is free.

More details on these and other Acts can be found in Chapter 13.

School procedures for monitoring and maintaining the supply of classroom resources and your role and responsibility in relation to this

Each school will have its own procedures for monitoring and maintaining the supply of resources for the classroom. You will need to familiarise yourself with these. Your role in the process should be explained to you by the teachers you are working with or the SENCO.

Checklist

- ✔ I am familiar with the procedures for keeping records in my school.
- ✔ I know which type of records are kept in the school office and which are kept in the classrooms.
- ✔ I am familiar with IEPs and understand their structure and purpose.
- ✔ I understand the necessity of ensuring that all records are accurate and kept up to date.
- ✔ I understand the need for confidentiality and am familiar with the procedures in my school for guarding that confidentiality.
- ✔ I am aware of legislation relating to record keeping.

MEETING PERFORMANCE INDICATORS

2.1.1 Help with the organisation of the learning environment: checking the availability of safety equipment

Setting the scene

As part of her induction to the post of teaching assistant, Miranda is taken on a tour of the school by the administration officer. One focus of the tour is the features of health and safety with which she is required to become familiar.

Writing personal accounts: covering performance indicators

As Miranda has enrolled on an NVQ 2 teaching assistant course she can use this tour of the school as evidence; but how?

First, when writing up what she has seen and done, Miranda needs to make reference to the following performance indicator. Remember the tips on writing personal accounts (page 8) – look at the standards first.

Unit 2.1.1 Help with the organisation of the learning environment: checking the availability of safety equipment

Performance indicator	*Scope of safety equipment*	*Scope of learning environment*
(2) Check the availability and location of *safety equipment* in the *learning environment.*	(a) First aid box	(a) General teaching area (b) Specialist teaching area (c) Outdoor area
	(b) Equipment to protect children and adults against accidents	(a) General teaching area (b) Specialist teaching area (c) Outdoor area
	(c) Equipment for use in an emergency	(a) General teaching area (b) Specialist teaching area (c) Outdoor area

Miranda could have submitted something like this:

Personal Account: Miranda Appleton

I went round the school with Mrs Biggins and saw the first aid boxes, the fire extinguishers and the fire blanket. I saw where the medicines are kept and where the fire alarms are. I found out how adults and children are kept safe in the kitchen, hall and ICT suite as well as in the classroom. I found out what to do in an emergency.

Although this is an accurate account of what happened, Miranda needs to write a much fuller account to show that she really understands and knows what to do in an emergency situation.

Personal Account

Name: Miranda Appleton
Date: 15 September 2005
2.1.1 Help with the organisation of the learning environment

Safety equipment and emergency procedures

I was taken on a tour of the school by Mrs Biggins, the administration officer, to check the availability and location of safety equipment in the learning environment (2.1.1)

The school office

First of all she showed me what was held in the school office itself:

This is much more detailed!

- An Emergency Procedures ring binder containing plans of the school showing the gas points, the water stopcocks, the position of all fire extinguishers, fire blankets and fire alarms, and the position of electrical cut-off points. In the event of electrical failure, gas leak or flooding it is clear where the relevant equipment is to isolate the danger.
- An emergency is anything which puts the safety of the school (both pupils and staff) at risk. I was informed that, as our school is close to a naval dockyard where ships from many nations berth, we have been issued with anti-radiation tablets which are stored in a locked cupboard in the caretaker's room. In the event of a radiation warning to be issued by the emergency services, these tablets will be unlocked and distributed by the administration staff, the head teacher or deputy head teacher.

Checked equipment to protect children and adults against accidents: 2.1.1 2b

- A lockable cupboard where medicines are kept for specific pupils who may need to take them in school. These include asthma inhalers, insulin syringes with a yellow box for 'sharps' (used needles which need to be kept secure and separate from everything else). There are also two EpiPens® which are syringes already loaded with medicine. They are for a pupil who is severely allergic to nuts and may suffer anaphylactic shock if he comes into contact with them. There is a list of all pupils who may require these medicines displayed in the cupboard. The list of all pupils with possible medical issues is kept in the main Pupil Record file in the office desk. The administration officer, the head teacher and the deputy head teacher have keys to the lockable cupboard. Nobody else has access to it.
- Administering these medicines – all three office staff have been trained in 'First Aid at Work' and all have been specifically trained in the administration of these medicines.

Checked first aid box: 2.1.1 2a

- First aid box – in a quiet room adjacent to the actual school office I was shown the locked first aid box. Again, the keys are held only by the administration officer, the head teacher and deputy head teacher. The first aid box contains disinfectant wipes, plasters (a list of pupils allergic to plasters is held in the school office), various bandages and safety pins, safety scissors, sterile dressings and a laminated sheet outlining common first aid procedures. Next to the first aid box is a box of latex disposable gloves. Inside the first aid box is a note regarding one pupil who is allergic to latex. Within the quiet room there is also a pile of disposable cardboard bowls to be used when pupils feel they are going to be sick. If pupils actually are sick in them, the office staff dispose of the bowls and the contents in a specially marked yellow plastic bag. The staff wear disposable latex gloves all the time they are handling these bowls.

I was then taken on a tour of the school as a whole:

- First aid equipment is held in the school office – the classrooms do not have separate first aid boxes. The school does, however, own two minibuses, and there is a fully equipped first aid box in each of these buses. There are also a couple of smaller first aid boxes kept in the school office ready to be taken on school trips.

Checked the availability and location of safety equipment in the general teaching area: 2.1.1 2c

General learning environment

- Fire extinguishers are placed outside several of the classrooms and outside the kitchen area. In conversation both with Mrs Biggins and the school caretaker, it was generally agreed that, in the event of a fire, the first priority would be to evacuate the school rather than attempt to use fire extinguishers to fight it.
- Fire alarms are located near each exit and in the middle of the longer corridors. There is also one immediately outside the kitchen. These are enclosed in glass cases which must be broken using a small hammer attached to the wall beside the alarms. The alarms and fire extinguishers are all checked annually by the fire service. Fire drills are held termly in the school on different days and at different times. They are logged in the 'Emergency Procedures' file.

You show you are aware of whole school policies and procedures.

Specific teaching areas

- Kitchen area – there is a sand bucket near the door and a fire blanket fixed to the wall beside the oven. Over the sink there is a yellow sign with black writing warning that the water is hot.
- ICT suite – the ICT manager pointed out the safety features of the ICT suite: all towers are secured within cupboards beneath the monitors and keyboards; all cables between towers, monitors and keyboards are protected by coiled plastic which prevents tangling of cables and protects the cables from any interference; all batteries, spare cables and plugs are kept in a

lockable cupboard; all laptops are kept in a different lockable cupboard in the ICT suite along with their cables and transformers. The keys to these cupboards are kept in the school office.
- Fire safety – when ascending the stairs to the second floor I was informed that the space under the stairs needs to be kept clear as it is a potential fire hazard.

Good to see you appreciate that safety applies to both staff and pupils.

- The school hall is used for PE and has wall bars, horses, mats, benches and a range of climbing equipment. Mrs Biggins told me that all teachers have been trained in the appropriate use of this equipment, particularly in setting them out. Children are taught how to carry the mats and equipment safely and how to use them safely.

Outdoor area

- External security – the school has two main entrances. The one at the rear is to let vehicles in and is locked half an hour after the beginning of the school day and not unlocked until near the end of the day. The school office staff and the caretaker have the keys to this gate, which can be unlocked to let in emergency vehicles if need be. Anyone needing to drive out of school during the day needs to log their use of the key in the school office. The main front entrance has a security code known only to the staff. Any visitor needs to buzz through the intercom to the school office and the staff there will check their status and purpose of their visit before letting them in.
- Disability issues – all stairs inside the school and steps outside the school have the noses of their treads painted yellow to give greater visibility. Ramps have been built up to the main entrances of the actual building.
- Safety when moving around the school – Mrs Biggins pointed out the hanging spaces for coats and the boxes for bags and lunch boxes. The aim is to avoid clutter in the corridors so that pupils can move about safely. This is particularly pertinent as there is one pupil in the school with a visual impairment.

General teaching areas

Finally Mrs Biggins showed me each of the classrooms:

- All cables are, wherever possible, secured to the walls out of the way of children. Where cables do need to be laid across the floor – such as electrical leads from sockets to the overhead projector – they are covered with heavy rubber strips to keep them flat.
- Each classroom has wooden racks in which to place scissors, points downward.
- As the school is a primary school, there is no separate science laboratory or design and technology (DT) room; however, there is a central supply of goggles to be worn by pupils if they are involved in activities which may have an element of danger.
- The school has a policy of ensuring all classrooms are kept tidy and uncluttered, so that all equipment is put away in trays, boxes or cupboards after they have been used.

Administration officer's comments

I certify that this is a true statement of what occurred.

Staff signature	Name (printed and role)
M Biggins	Mabel Biggins, Administration Officer

Assessor's comments

This is an extremely detailed personal account. I really get the sense that you know where everything is and what the procedures are for any eventuality. Well done. My only comment is that you could have written in the right-hand margin where you specifically met an indicator. I have done this for you. I have written out what indicators you have covered as well as stating the appropriate numbers. As you become more experienced in writing personal accounts, you will be able to do this for yourself. Some candidates use the performance indicators as subheadings to structure their work.

As part of your evidence you could also include a drawing of this school highlighting where safety equipment is kept.

Not only can this personal account be used as evidence against performance indicators, but also it can be used as evidence towards the knowledge base for this unit – specifically what safety equipment is kept in the different learning environments. I will still need additional information from you in regard to your school's health and safety policy.

Signed: Terrie Cole
Terrie Cole
NVQ Assessor

Another way of presenting evidence

It is important to remember that there are many ways of presenting evidence. Miranda could have presented some of her evidence in the form of a checklist such as the one below, which has been partially completed. A blank template can be found in the Appendix at the end of this book.

What can be found in a first aid box?

Equipment	*Seen*	*Comments*	*Witnessed by*
Scissors	6.1.06	Points covered in plastic guard to prevent injury	M Biggins Admin Officer
Guidance card	6.1.06	Outlines response to common injuries and accidents – useful aide-memoire but nothing more	M Biggins Admin Officer
Safety pins			
Disposable gloves			
Sterile coverings			
Individual sterile dressings			
Cloth triangular bandage			
Medium dressings			
Large dressings			
Eye pad			

2.1.1 Help with the organisation of the learning environment: the learning resources and materials

Setting the scene

A Year 2 literacy lesson – the pupils are to write alternative endings to familiar stories. Miranda has been asked to rearrange the classroom slightly while the pupils are in assembly in order for them to better access the lesson. The teacher has shown her what learning materials need to be set out. At the end of the lesson she helps the pupils tidy up.

Writing personal accounts: covering performance indicators

When writing up what she has seen and done, Miranda needs to make reference to the performance indicators on page 27.

In writing this personal account, Miranda can refer only to what actually happened in the particular instance of setting up for a Year 2 literacy lesson in class. She can make no reference to a learning environment other than a general teaching area.

She will need to provide additional evidence to show she meets these performance indicators in other teaching areas.

She needs to distinguish between the three types of materials identified in the performance indicators – *general classroom items*, *curriculum specific materials* and *written materials*. As she is describing a writing lesson, this poses some difficulty as the 'curriculum specific' materials *are* 'written materials'. Other types of lesson make it easier to distinguish between the two. Had she been describing a numeracy activity, for instance, she could have made reference to 'curriculum specific' materials such as number lines, dice and so on and to 'written materials' such as pens, pencils and worksheets.

Unit 2.1.1 Help with the organisation of the learning environment: learning resources and materials

Performance indicators	*Scope*
(1) Set out *learning resources* in line with the preparation requirements given to you.	(a) Basic classroom equipment and furniture (b) Curriculum specific equipment (c) ICT resources
(2) Set out *learning materials* as directed by the teacher.	(a) General classroom items (b) Curriculum specific materials (c) Written materials
(3) Report shortages of *learning materials* to the teacher.	(a) General classroom items (b) Curriculum specific materials (c) Written materials
(4) Encourage pupils to return *materials* to the appropriate place after use.	(a) General classroom items (b) Curriculum specific materials (c) Written materials
(5) Encourage pupils to dispose of waste in a safe and tidy manner.	
(6) Check the condition of *learning resources* and *materials* after use.	(a) Basic classroom equipment and furniture (b) Curriculum specific equipment (c) ICT resources (d) General classroom items (e) Curriculum specific materials (f) Written materials
(7) Bring any damage or losses to *learning resources* and *materials* to the attention of the teacher as soon as practicable.	(a) Basic classroom equipment and furniture (b) Curriculum specific equipment (c) ICT resources (d) General classroom items (e) Curriculum specific materials (f) Written materials

Personal Account

Name: Miranda Appleton
Date: 18 January 2006
2.1.1 Help with the organisation of the learning environment

The learning resources and materials

I set out the learning resources in line with the preparation requirements given to me.

Classroom considerations

I planned with the class teacher, Miss Peel, that, while the class were in assembly and she was setting up the interactive whiteboard in class, I would prepare the room for the literacy lesson. Not all pupils are able to see the teacher or the interactive whiteboard without craning their necks if they are seated at their normal places. This means that, for teacher input, they all sit on the carpet in front of her and the board. There is a visually impaired pupil in the class who needs to sit right in front of the teacher and the interactive whiteboard when it is being used. If she is on a slant to the screen she finds it very difficult to see. However, she is also light sensitive so, when she is working independently, she needs to sit so she is not facing a constant light source.

Set out the learning resources (basic classroom equipment and furniture)

I moved two tables to make room for the whole class to sit in front of Miss Peel and the whiteboard screen when she began the lesson. Following her input I pushed the tables back to their original position so that all pupils had a place to sit and were able to move freely around the room.

Set out ICT resources

While Miss Peel set up her laptop computer, connecting it to the interactive whiteboard projector, I turned on the four classroom desktop computers and made sure the required software was available for a group of pupils to use later in the lesson.

Finally, I rehearsed areas of potential accidents – noting that wires from the laptop to the interactive whiteboard were out of the way, secured to the wall; all scissors were in their racks; the fire exits were clear. I noted that there was a fire extinguisher in the corridor right outside the door to the classroom. The first aid box is in the school office across the courtyard.

Set out the learning materials as directed by the teacher (curriculum specific materials and written materials)

The class were using writing frames to help them generate alternative endings to familiar stories. Three days before the lesson I had, in line with school procedures, asked the office staff to photocopy enough writing frames for each pupil in the class. I collected these from the office first thing in the morning, then, during the assembly, I distributed the writing frames and pencils to each place. Before giving out the pencils I made sure they had been sharpened. I ensured that each group of tables had a word bank of high frequency words available to use.

I then set up the sloping board for the visually impaired child and ensured she had an enlarged writing frame. I also set out several triangular pencils for pupils experiencing difficulty with handwriting.

Just before the pupils returned to class I had all the small personal whiteboards and dry wipe markers ready to distribute as they came in.

Include this notification as supplementary evidence

Reported shortages

During the lesson it became apparent that more pupils could do with using triangular pencils. Later in the day I notified the Special Educational Needs Coordinator of this so that more can be ordered via the school office.

Encouraged pupils to return materials to appropriate place after use

At the end of the teacher input I supervised the children putting their personal whiteboards and markers into the appropriate boxes as they went to their places.

At the end of the lesson I checked that all pupils followed the class routine of returning pencils, rubbers and pencil sharpeners into a tub at the centre of each group. I helped collect up the work, placing completed or partially completed work into Miss Peel's tray for marking. I gathered up any unused paper and placed it back in the store cupboard in the classroom.

Encouraged pupils to dispose of waste in a safe and tidy manner

There was not much mess at the end of this lesson – not like art anyway! During the lesson I made sure that pupils who had sharpened their pencils had placed the sharpenings in the bin rather than scatter them on the floor. At the end of the lesson I told a couple of pupils to pick up pencils they had dropped on the floor under their desks. I also needed to ask some pupils to pick up pieces of paper they had crumpled up and left on the floor. In doing this I was enforcing the general classroom routines which all the pupils are familiar with.

Checked the condition of the learning resources and materials after use

During the lesson I checked that the materials the pupils had to work with were of a sufficient standard – for instance, that the writing frames had been photocopied properly and were not torn or indistinct. At the end of the lesson, I noted that several pencils were breaking regularly and were becoming worn down with constant sharpening. I spoke to Miss Peel about this as we were clearing away and she asked me to get some new ones from the stock room. I did this later in the day. I also saw that the paper strimmer had become damaged – the cutter blade had come loose and was becoming a danger. I showed this to Miss Peel and she took it to the office to be repaired.

Teacher's comments

I was very appreciative of Miranda's help and noted how well everything was prepared in the way I asked.

I certify that this is a true statement of what occurred.

Teacher's signature	Name (printed and role)
J Peel	Jane Peel, Class Teacher

Assessor's comments

A very detailed personal account in which you clearly demonstrate how you have helped in organising the learning environment. Well done.

I note that you are using performance indicators as subheadings. Again, well done! You have included much evidence in one account. You could try and use a diary approach as I am sure you do this every day. As I noted, do you have supplementary evidence of reporting shortages and damage to equipment? If so, include this as part of your evidence.

Signed: Terrie Cole
Terrie Cole
NVQ Assessor

Nicola, the secondary school TA, collected evidence of reporting shortages and noting breakages in a diary method. A photocopiable blank copy is to be found in the Appendix (page 202).

The learning resources and materials

Resources	*Seen*	*Used*	*Witness (name and title)*
General stock cupboard	17.5.06	17.5.06 As per school policy, I signed the stock cupboard key out of school office, unlocked the store cupboard, collected 30 exercise books and two boxes of pens for the class, locked the cupboard and returned the key to the office.	M. Henley 17.5.06 Admin Officer
ICT – software and hardware			
Maths			
Literacy			
Science, including environmental resources			
Design and technology			
Art	26.4.06	26.4.06 I collected boxes of coloured chalks and two packs of cartridge paper from the art cupboard outside the school office to use in the lesson this afternoon.	Dennis Watson 26.4.06 Head of art department

The learning resources and materials (continued)

Resources	*Seen*	*Used*	*Witness (name and title)*
Music			
PE			
History			
Geography			
RE (Religious education)			
PSHE (Personal, social and health education)			
Local studies	12.5.06	12.5.06 I collected maps of the local area from the Environ-mental Studies section of the geography resources cupboard outside the hall.	Anne Jamieson 12.5.06 Geography Teacher
Other (specify)			

2.1.2 Help with classroom records

Setting the scene

As part of her support in the Year 2 literacy lesson, as described in Unit 2.1.1 (the class writing alternative endings to familiar stories), Miranda completes class records as the lesson draws to a close. She focuses on five pupils who have writing targets in their IEPs, one of whom is the pupil with the visual impairment.

Writing personal accounts: covering performance indicators

When writing up what she has seen and done, Miranda needs to make reference to the following performance indicators:

When writing up her personal accounts, Miranda should not feel she has to cover all the performance indicators in one go. She is likely to need a separate account for keeping records of out-of-school activities. In the following account she focuses on records kept within the classroom.

Unit 2.1.2 Help with classroom records

Performance indicators	*Scope*
(1) Complete *records* accurately and legibly with the details specified by the teacher.	(a) Relating to pupil progress (b) Relating to out-of-school activities (c) Relating to the availability and supply of classroom resources
(2) Update individual pupil *records* under direction from the teacher.	(a) Relating to pupil progress (b) Relating to out-of-school activities (c) Relating to the availability and supply of classroom resources
(3) Comply with the school requirements for storage and security of pupil *records* at all times.	(a) Relating to pupil progress (b) Relating to out-of-school activities (c) Relating to the availability and supply of classroom resources
(4) Make sure that information for the school office is collected, collated and passed on as promptly as possible.	(a) Relating to pupil progress (b) Relating to out-of-school activities (c) Relating to the availability and supply of classroom resources
(5) Maintain confidentiality according to organisational and legal requirements.	(a) Relating to pupil progress (b) Relating to out-of-school activities (c) Relating to the availability and supply of classroom resources

Personal Account

Name: Miranda Appleton
Date: 21 February 2006
2.1.2 Help with classroom records

You need to explain what these terms mean.

General comments

As a school we have begun to develop our marking and record keeping in line with 'Assessment for Learning' whereby marking and recording becomes 'formative' rather than 'summative' in order to help the pupils make progress in their learning. Miss Peel asked me before the lesson if I would record the progress made by the five pupils who have writing targets on their IEPs. She asked me if I would do this during the course of the lesson so that I could talk with the pupils as I marked their work.

Each class in the school has an assessment folder containing a 'Pupil Profile' for every member of the class, which is simply sheets of paper on which records of progress, contact with parents and any areas of concern are made. Miss Peel asked if I would write on the profiles for each of the five pupils two things – to what extent they were achieving the learning objective (something which is common to the whole class) and to what extent were they achieving their IEP targets (specific to the individual pupils concerned). One of the pupils with an IEP for writing is the pupil with the visual impairment.

In order to record pupil progress accurately I needed to look at their work and to talk with them, asking them questions about it. Part of my recording was to note down whether the learning task was too easy, too hard or was an appropriate level for these pupils. I also needed to comment on the suitability of the additional resources provided for the visually impaired pupil.

This is very good evidence – you need to include a copy of these records.

Completed records accurately and legibly with details specified by teacher

Towards the end of the lesson I took the appropriate pupil records from the class assessment file. I wrote the date, the time and the lesson on each of the Pupil Profiles.

I went to the group where five pupils have some level of special educational need and have IEPs with targets relating to writing. I encouraged them by commenting on the hard work they had done, then asked to look at each of their work. I wrote down on each Pupil Profile to what extent, in my judgement, they had achieved the learning objective.

I also asked them if they remembered their 'special target' which, for most, was correctly spelling the NLS List 1 high frequency words. I opened the ring binder at the IEPs, wrote the date and noted how far the pupils had achieved their targets in this piece of work.

Most had achieved the learning objective, but I noted on one Pupil Profile that he had not understood the activity and had written about what he had done at the weekend. Afterwards I added a written note that this pupil often confuses his tasks.

I particularly checked on the child with the visual impairment – noting that the sloping board had been useful in helping her write her story ending and that the enlarged writing frame was useful in helping her read. I wrote that she would have found it difficult to access the activity if she had been given the same size print as everyone else.

At the end of my recording I printed and signed my name so that others reading it should know who had entered this particular information.

Complied with the school requirements for storage and security of pupil records at all times

After the lesson I placed the pupil records back in the class assessment file and replaced the file on the shelf in Miss Peel's cupboard out of the reach of children. Later Miss Peel looked at it and discussed with me the concerns over the pupil who misunderstood the task. She thanked me for the detail of my observations and for the fact that they were legible!

This links to knowledge base requirements.

The class assessment file only contains information regarding pupil progress. In keeping with school policy, anything of a more confidential nature, such as attendance, sickness records and issues of child protection, is held in lockable files in the school office. The SENCO also keeps records of pupils on the SEN Register, again in a lockable filing cabinet.

Made sure that information for the school office is collected, collated and passed on as promptly as possible

Can you give me evidence of this?

Although in this lesson there was no information to be collected directly for the school office, I have done this on other occasions. As part of my role in supporting Miss Peel, I collect money for school trips if they occur and also organise children's forms for school photographs.

My observations regarding meeting IEP targets have been used in IEP reviews held between Miss Peel, the SENCO and myself and were shared with parents by Miss Peel at parents' evenings. My assessment of whether the children have achieved their learning objectives has contributed towards Miss Peel's 'teacher assessment'. I pass the information to her and she uses this to help give the children a National Curriculum level for writing. This information is collated by the school office staff and kept by them in a central file. Ultimately statistics from these records are given to the governors and to the local authority.

This links with knowledge base requirements.

Maintained confidentiality according to organisational and legal requirements

I talked about the records I wrote with Miss Peel and with the SENCO, but I am aware that confidentiality is important. I did not talk about them with any parents or with members of staff not involved with the children.

Teacher's comments

Miranda was a real support in class.
I certify that this is a true statement of what occurred.

Teacher's signature	Name (printed and role)
J Peel	Jane Peel, Class Teacher

Assessor's comments

Again, Miranda, a very good piece of evidence. You make reference to the notes you have written regarding the pupils. Can you include this as supporting evidence in your portfolio? Remember confidentiality and block out all their names.

Instead of writing a personal account, you could have just included copies of pupil records with a brief note regarding how you filled these in. Here you are talking about Pupil Profiles, but you could have mentioned filling in reading diaries which you do on a day-to-day basis.

You mention that as part of your role you collect money for school trips. I am sure that you do, but you need to provide me with witnessed evidence of this. You could collect this evidence as part of the diary method:

For example:

Date	Event	Witnessed
9 March 2006	I collected money for class trip to local museum, passing the money to the school office.	

Some of what you write – formative and summative assessment, procedures for record-keeping – demonstrates underpinning knowledge. I will need to ask you more details about this.

Signed: Terrie Cole

Terrie Cole

NVQ Assessor

Chapter 3

Unit 2.2 Help with the care and support of pupils

In this unit there are two elements:

2.2.1 Help with the care and support of individual pupils
2.2.2 Help with the care and support of groups of pupils

KNOWLEDGE BASE

2.2.1 and 2.2.2 Help with the care and support of individual pupils and groups of pupils

The role required of you in supporting individual pupils

A TA's role in supporting pupils will be summarised in your job description. Most job descriptions will state that:

- You will assist the teacher in implementing the lesson plans. Specifically you will work with the pupils assigned to you and help them to meet the **learning objectives** as outlined by the teacher.
- Schools are not just about learning academic facts, they are also about developing social and emotional skills. As a TA you need to develop a good relationship with the pupils you support, as well as helping and encouraging them to develop positive relationships with each other. In doing this you will teach pupils how to manage conflicts and how to deal with their emotions positively.
- As a TA you will have high expectations in regard to achievement and behaviour. You can help a pupil by reminding them of what they are supposed to be doing and encouraging and praising them for their efforts.
- As a TA you are not there to do the work for them, rather you are there to help them to learn to do the work for themselves. You can help pupils set clear goals for themselves. In order to do this you need to be able to talk to the pupil in a way that they can understand.
- As a TA you will feedback to the teacher regarding how the session went. For example you will need to make comments on: who could do the work; who found the work difficult; who would benefit from extra time or help in that area; who was disruptive and who was very supportive and encouraging to their fellow pupils.

School policies for inclusion

Those involved in the field of education often talk about **inclusion.** The aim of inclusion is that all children or pupils, regardless of abilities, disabilities or special educational needs (SEN), are educated together in age-appropriate mainstream local schools. For inclusion to work and for pupils with special educational needs to experience success the school will need to be given the required support and resources.

Inclusion is more than integration. Integration is about location. When I was at school, a long time ago, there was a classroom, where all the children with special needs in the school went. I never knew these pupils. In a sense that was integration. Pupils with special needs attended my school but they were separate.

Inclusion means that all pupils are involved in all aspects of school life. Inclusion is about creating relationships and valuing differences. Inclusion sets out values that should be evident in all that happens within a school. Schools will state how they will promote equal opportunities and disability awareness in school policy documents. As a TA it is useful to see these policies. As a TA enrolled on an NVQ 2 course it is important that you obtain a copy of these policies and that you read them. When schools write their policies they refer to guidance from local authorities and government documents.

Legislation regarding inclusion

Inclusive education is enshrined in law – notably by the Children Act 1989, the various Education Acts of the 1990s, the Special Education Needs and Disability Act 2001, the Children Act 2004 and the Disability Discrimination Act 2005. More details on these and other pieces of legislation are given in Chapter 13. Schools have a legal requirement not to discriminate against pupils with disabilities and are required to make provision for them. Plans must be put in place to make every school accessible to persons with disabilities. No school can refuse to admit a pupil on the grounds that they feel unable to meet their needs.

For a school to be inclusive all those involved in the school must continually work towards these values on a day-to-day basis. As a TA you have a role to play.

Individual Educational Plans

In meeting the needs of pupils, schools will follow the *Special Educational Needs Code of Practice* (Department for Education and Employment (DfEE) 2001). The Code of Practice is a government document that outlines levels of intervention that the school will follow.

Monitoring (early identification)

Monitoring is an unofficial first step. This is where the school will keep an eye on a specific pupil. It could be that the pupil is having problems with reading, writing or maths. At this stage the child will receive **differentiated** work, which is work that is set for the pupil's specific ability.

School action

If there is still concern for the pupil, after receiving differentiated learning opportunities, the pupil is put on the school's Special Educational Needs Register. This concern could be one of the following:

- Pupil is making little or no progress even with differentiated work.
- Pupil shows signs of difficulty in literacy or maths that could affect their work in other subject areas.
- Pupil has ongoing emotional and behavioural problems that are not being dealt with by existing school behaviour management techniques.
- Pupil has sensory or physical difficulties and even with specialist equipment is making little or no progress.
- Pupil has communication and/or interaction difficulties and makes little or no progress despite differentiated learning opportunities.

Once the pupil is on the SEN Register, at the School Action Stage, the SENCO will collect all available information, seek new information and carry out further assessment. The result of this will be the formulation of an Individual Educational Plan (IEP). An IEP will outline the support the pupil will be given. Specifically an IEP will outline:

- Short-term targets.
- Teaching strategies.
- Provisions to be put into place.
- When the plan should be reviewed.
- What the pupil needs to do to meet the targets: this has been called the success or exit criteria.
- A review of the IEP, that is, whether the pupil has met the targets.

School action plus

If after receiving an individualised programme of support, which is described in the IEP, the pupil still is making little or no progress, the pupil can move to the next level of intervention. At this point the school will ask for help and support from outside agencies. This could include behaviour support team, speech and language therapists or educational psychologists.

Statement of Special Educational Need

If after receiving help from outside agencies it is felt that the pupil is not making adequate progress then the school in discussion with the parents and external agencies can ask the local authority to implement a statutory assessment. The educational psychologist will be involved and if it is felt that the pupil is still not making progress a Statement of Special Educational Need is written (see page 191).

Code of Practice

The Code of Practice is said to be key in ensuring that inclusion happens in schools as it is committed to responding to pupils' diverse needs and to setting suitable learning challenges for all pupils. TAs will be involved on a day-to day basis in helping pupils meet their targets as stated on their IEPs. An example of an IEP is shown in the box.

Individual Educational Plan

Area of concern: Attention, literacy, behaviour

Name: Jody Smith
Stage: School Action
Year Group: Year 3
Start Date: Sept. 2005
Review Date: Jan. 2006
Support Began: Sept. 2005
Class Teacher: Mrs Gardner
Support by: Miranda Appleton TA

Targets to be achieved	*Achievement criteria*	*Possible resources/ techniques*	*Possible class strategies*	*Ideas for teaching assistant*	*Outcome*
To speak politely to other pupils and adults	No incidents or rudeness for 3 days out of 5	• Clear expectations • All incidents of talking politely praised	• Discuss what is meant by being polite • Ignore minor episodes of rudeness	• Discuss what is polite behaviour in the classroom • Praise efforts • Use star chart	Incidents of rude-ness down from 5 a week to 2
To form all lower case letters accurately	Accurate in 2 pieces of work a week	• Guidelines on paper	• Ask Jody to write in her best for display purposes • Get Jody to rewrite her work if necessary	• Praise her for her efforts • Talk about the importance of accuracy and presenta-tion	Accurate in three pieces of work a week

Role of the TA required in promoting inclusion

- TAs can encourage all children, especially children with special educational needs to have a sense of pride in who they are.
- TAs can encourage friendships between all children.
- TAs can help pupils meet their targets as stated on their IEPs.
- TAs can challenge negative attitudes and low expectations. Did you know – it was only in the 1980s when reading intervention programmes for Down syndrome children were introduced that it was realised that children with Down syndrome could be taught to read?

- TAs can use strategies that help all pupils to develop their potential. Some specific strategies you can use include encouraging cooperation, helping pupils to recognise theirs and other's strengths, promoting independence and matching **teaching style** to **learning styles** (pages 57–9).

Specific strategies you can use to promote inclusion

Encouraging cooperation and effective interactions through praise

Cooperative learning techniques describe ways to help pupils work together. For example a group of pupils may be working on a presentation regarding 'Life in Victorian times'. A well-known cooperative learning technique has been referred to as the jigsaw technique or jigsaw classroom (Aronson and Patnoe 1997). The jigsaw technique goes like this:

- Pupils are divided into groups. Groups should be diverse in terms of bringing together pupils from different cultural backgrounds and different levels of ability.
- The task is divided into segments. Each pupil is given responsibility for one segment. For example if the group task was to write about the life of The Victorians, the segments could include: Family Life, Work Life, The Government, The Royal Family and Transport. Each pupil would be responsible for one segment or one piece of the puzzle.
- The pupils are then asked to form expert groups with other pupils who are working on the same segment or piece of the puzzle. For example all those pupils who are working on the Royal Family would come together to research the topic.
- After the pupils have worked with their expert groups they are then asked to come back to the main group and present their findings. The other group members are encouraged to ask questions.

The jigsaw strategy is just one technique that can be used in a classroom. The advantage is that it encourages children of varying abilities to work and cooperate with each other. In these group tasks pupils are required to

- contribute their ideas to the discussion
- listen to others' ideas
- give every member of the group an opportunity to speak
- value each other's contributions
- ask each other for help before asking the teacher or teaching assistant to intervene
- try to settle arguments among themselves.

These group requirements can be presented to the pupils as guidelines or rules for helping them work together.

However, for groups to work effectively they will need guidance and help from teachers and teaching assistants. In groups you can have difficulties with various kinds of pupils:

- pupils who like to dominate the group
- free-riders who do not contribute and let others do the work for them

- less able pupils who struggle to keep up
- able pupils who may get bored
- needy pupils who are making constant demands on your attention.

TAs can help by reminding pupils of what they need to do to work together. TAs can praise pupils for doing this. Remember praise encourages cooperation and effective interactions. In relation to less able pupils, it is important to give them a task that they can do. Perhaps you could ask a more able pupil to assist a less able pupil. In helping a less able pupil, the more able pupil also benefits as the skills involved in explaining work to others helps to consolidate their own understanding.

Helping to find value in everyone: multiple intelligence

Encouraging pupils to notice and value what other pupils can do well encourages positive interactions and cooperation between pupils. Traditionally pupils in schools have been valued for academic successes. This can result in competition between some pupils for the highest marks. It is possible that pupils who think that they can not compete and that they never will get the highest marks could label themselves as 'thick' and just give up.

The theory of multiple intelligence (Gardner 1993) criticises the notion that intelligence is just about academic success. This theory states that there are different types of intelligence and that society needs individuals with different types of intelligence (see Figure 3.1).

Figure 3.1 TAs need to look for talent in all pupils

Types of intelligence	*Pupils' skills and talents*
Logical-mathematical	This pupil has a flair for maths. A pupil with this type of intelligence is good at performing calculations and analysing how things work. Future careers could include engineers, computer scientists, accountants and analysts.
Linguistic	This pupil excels at written work. This pupil is naturally good with words and using language, enjoys writing stories and commenting on others' work. Future careers could include journalists, linguists, writers and lawyers.
Musical	This pupil has a flair for music, sound and rhythm. This pupil could be good at singing or playing a musical instrument or teaching another pupil how to sing or play a musical instrument. Future careers could include musicians, singers, composers and disk jockeys.
Bodily-kinaesthetic	This pupil has good body movement control. This pupil is physically agile and has good coordination. This pupil could be good at sports and also at demonstrating physical skills to others. Future careers include dancers, athletes, soldiers, firefighters and divers.
Spatial-visual	This pupil is good at creating and understanding visual images and shapes. This pupil could be good at painting, designing logos and drawing maps. Future careers include artists, designers, architects, photographers and town planners.
Interpersonal	This pupil is good with people. This pupil can easily understand other people's feelings. Future careers could include counsellors, psychologists, clergy and sales people.
Intrapersonal	This pupil is good at self-awareness, that is, good at understanding why they do what they do. Self-awareness is an essential part of what is now termed emotional intelligence.

How to provide support for a pupil while encouraging independence

Inclusion involves encouraging pupils to interact with each other in a positive manner. Inclusion also involves creating learning opportunities that pupils can participate in. It is easy to fall into the trap of doing the work for a pupil who is struggling. However, if you did this then the pupil would not be learning. If you did the pupil's work for them then the teacher would find it difficult to know exactly what the pupil can do by themselves. As a TA you need to give the pupil the skills so that they can learn for themselves (Figure 3.2).

It is easy to fall into the trap of allowing the pupil to become dependent on you. This is the pupil who would always prefer to be with you at break time rather than being with their peers. Some pupils struggle in relating to the other pupils in their class, but your role involves helping them to relate to others.

Stephanie Lorenz (2002) talks about three different types of TAs:

> There is the TA that is Velcro'd to the pupils they support. They are stuck to them like glue. However this way of working with a pupil does not allow the pupil to relate to others in their class. In fact this approach can make a pupil even more isolated. Some pupils may dislike this type of support as they may start to feel different from everyone else.
>
> The next type of TA has been compared to a hovering helicopter, the TA is always at hand if anything is to go wrong or the pupil needs help. This approach is better

Figure 3.2 TAs need to encourage independence

than the 'Velcro'd approach' however sometimes pupils need space and time to try and work things out for themselves. Sometimes it is important for pupils to make mistakes. It is a fact of life that we often learn more when things go wrong. However, in saying that, often pupils will need a TA's help in realising that making mistakes is not the end of the world and that they can actually help you to learn.

The next type of TA is called a bridge builder – this type of TA creates with the teacher learning opportunities that the pupil can do and creates opportunities where the pupil can interact in a positive manner with other pupils.

Basic principles of effective communication and interaction with pupils

The diagram, on page 44, illustrates several important ways of communicating effectively with pupils.

The importance of adults as role models and the implications of this for my behaviour

Children and adults learn in many ways. One way of learning involves imitation – that is, you watch what someone else is doing and then you decide to try this yourself. This method of learning is referred to as the **social learning theory**. To learn by imitation a pupil needs to

- pay attention to what someone else is doing
- remember what that person has done

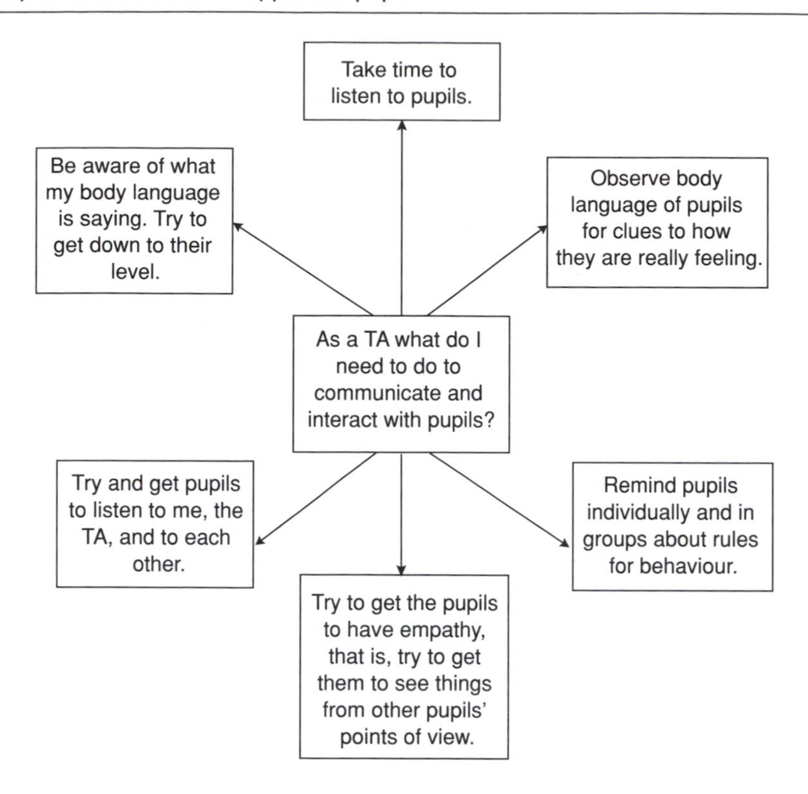

- be motivated to want to imitate the behaviour (pupils are more likely to imitate a behaviour if they see someone being rewarded for the behaviour)
- have the skills to perform the behaviour.

As a teaching assistant you can be a role model. You can demonstrate behaviour that you would like pupils to copy. This can be simple things such as remembering to say please and thank you and holding doors open for others to pass. It can also be talking to other members of staff in a respectful manner. As a TA you also need to reward or praise others when you see them behaving appropriately. Remember – a pupil is more likely to imitate what someone else is doing if they see that person being rewarded for that behaviour.

Difficulties that might arise in interacting effectively with a pupil and how to deal with these

In this chapter we have talked at length about how to interact effectively with pupils. To test your knowledge have a go at filling in the following table. If you do this you will be able to use this as evidence for knowledge base indicators. To help you get started a few examples have been given. A photocopiable template for this is in the Appendix.

Difficulties that might arise in interacting effectively with a pupil and how to deal with these	*Ways that I could deal with these*
Pupils who always want me to do the work for them.	I need to encourage pupils to become independent learners. To begin I could help them but slowly over time I would help them less and less and expect them to do more and more of the task by themselves.
Pupils who find it difficult to pay attention.	When working with the younger pupils I can remind them that they need to pay attention with their eyes, their ears and their hands. If they have targets regarding paying attention on their IEP, I will read the IEP so I know the strategies that I could use to help them.
Pupils who always want to have things their way.	
Pupils who feel they are not as good as other pupils.	
Pupils who make fun of other pupils who are struggling with their work.	
Pupils who refuse to do what I ask them.	

Checklist

- ✔ I make time to feedback to the teacher.
- ✔ I am familiar with the IEPs of the pupils I support.
- ✔ I do all that I can to encourage inclusion.
- ✔ I encourage pupils to become independent learners.

MEETING PERFORMANCE INDICATORS

2.2.1 Help with the care and support of individual pupils

Setting the scene

Nicola works in a secondary school. Nicola writes up one session as a personal account to cover Unit 2. Nicola remembers the advice of her assessor, Terrie, and looks at the standards she hopes to cover before writing up the account.

Unit 2.2.1 Help with the care and support of individual pupils

Performance indicator	*Scope*
(1) Provide the pupil with the level and type of individual attention specified by the teacher.	(a) Supporting with paying attention, concentrating and staying on task (b) Helping with tasks where there are physical difficulties, while encouraging independence and ensuring safety (c) Providing an escort for a pupil within and outside of the school
(2) Work to build a good relationship with the pupil.	
(3) Encourage the pupil to take responsibility for his/her own behaviour and to act independently.	
(4) Interact with the pupil in a manner appropriate to the pupil's communication and interaction skills.	

Personal Account

Name: Nicola Wilson
Date: 10 November 2005

I work in a secondary school with Year 9 pupils. One of the pupils I support on a regular basis has dyslexia, this means he has problems reading and writing. In addition to his dyslexia Rob (not his real name) has a slight problem with stammering. In some situations Rob is quite conscious of his stammer.

From previous discussions with the SENCO and the Head of English, I know that my role in regard to Rob is to

- help him with any written work
- to keep Rob on task
- to implement the learning strategies as outlined in his IEP
- encourage cursive writing.

On 10 November I was in an English class supporting Rob. I knew from conversation with the English teacher that the task was to write a campaign speech for one of the characters in *Animal*

Farm and deliver it to the rest of the class. I mentioned to her that I thought Rob would feel uncomfortable doing this due to his stammer. I suggested that perhaps he present his speech to the group. The teacher thought this was a good idea as Rob was in a particularly supportive group.

That session I worked with Rob in preparing his speech. I also offered support to the others in his group. We had previously watched a film about *Animal Farm* and Rob knew what he wanted to say. I praised Rob for his ideas and for concentrating on getting his speech together. I copied down what Rob said and then I asked Rob to copy his own version. This he did. He was a little nervous about reading his speech so I asked him to read the speech to me several times. I gave him lots of encouragement for his efforts. (Here I offered support with paying attention and staying on task 2.2.1 la.)

When it came to his turn to read out the speech in front of his group and the teacher it went extremely well. Both the teacher and I gave him lots of praise. I wrote out a special merit form for him.

Teacher's comments

Nicola worked very well in supporting Rob. I was very appreciative of her suggestion that Rob read out his speech in front of his group. In fact I put into place this strategy for the entire class and felt that all the pupils found this less daunting.

I certify that this is a true statement of what occurred.

Signed: M. Ames (Class Teacher)
Date: 11 November 2005

When Nicola submits this evidence to her assessor, she adds the following note to her assessor.

Dear Terrie,

I have written this about what happened today. I wanted to cover more performance indicators, but I have realised that I haven't done as much as I wanted to. It took me an hour to write this up! I will never get finished at this rate.

I am stuck on:
'working to build a good relationship with the pupil'
and
'encouraging the pupil to take responsibility for his/her own behaviour'
What does this mean? How can I show this?

Nicola

Assessor's comments

A good piece of evidence, Nicola.

It is hard to cover all performance indicators in one personal account. Remember personal accounts are just one type of evidence. Teachers can write witness statements and as your assessor I will go into your school on a regular basis and through observations help you to collect the information.

Working to build a good relationship with a pupil – It is very clear from reading between the lines that you have established a good relationship with Rob – but relationships with a pupil occur over time. You need to either cite more personal accounts of working with Rob or write a case study.

Encouraging the pupil to take responsibility for his/her own behaviour and to act independently

Well, behaviour could refer to 'paying attention and staying on task'. You know how sometimes some pupils would like you the TA to do all the work for them? You say you scribe for Rob. Do you scribe for all the pupils you support? Do you do this all the time? If you did this for the pupils – what would the pupils be doing?

I imagine that though you scribe for pupils sometimes, you also encourage them to take responsibility for staying on task and for doing as much of the work as they can – that is you encourage the pupils to act independently.

Taking responsibility for behaviour couldalso refer to incidents of inappropriate behaviour.

Some pupils will always follow the crowd, so if their mates are acting up, then they will too. In this case you could state choices and consequences. For example you could tell the pupil that if they continue to act up then you will tell the teacher and they will have to stay after school – or they can start to work – the choice is theirs.

Here the pupil would take responsibility for their behaviour and act independently of others.

You are right it is not always easy to understand what the performance indicators are asking you to do.

You mention that you are also working with Rob's group – but you do not mention any details regarding the group activity. Have a look at the indicators asking for evidence regarding **encouraging and reinforcing positive interactions between pupils** (2.2.2) before you next write up a personal account regarding a group activity.

As I said this personal account is a good piece of evidence and can be used to meet other performance indicators in other sections. Remember cross-referencing can cut down on the work you have to do for this course.

For example include a copy of the merit form you filled out for Rob as evidence for Unit 3.1 Contribute to the management of pupil behaviour.

Your suggestions regarding how individuals should present their speeches and your teacher's comments about how valuable your suggestion was can be used as evidence for Unit 2.3 Provide support for learning activities and Unit 2.4 Provide effective support for colleagues.

Signed: Terrie Cole

Terrie Cole
NVQ Assessor

Unit 2.2.2 Help with the care and support of groups of pupils

Nicola, before writing the next account, looked at the standards for Unit 2.2.2.

Unit 2.2.2 Help with the care and support of groups of pupils

Performance indicators	*Scope*
(1) Encourage and reinforce positive interaction between pupils.	(a) Between pairs (b) Within groups of three or more (c) With peers (d) With younger pupils (e) With pupils from different backgrounds and cultures
(2) Encourage groups to work together to comply with targets they have been set.	(a) In relation to classroom discipline (b) In relation to behaviour within and behaviour outside of school premises
(3) Consistently demonstrate respect for the rights of others in your own interactions with pupils and other adults.	
(4) Monitor the group's behaviour attentively enough to spot any signs of conflict or dangerous actions at an early stage.	
(5) Respond to conflict situations and incidents of antisocial behaviour in line with school policies and within the scope of your own responsibilities.	Racist Sexist Abusive in other ways
(6) Seek the assistance of appropriate staff where conflicts or antisocial behaviour occur that are outside of your role to resolve.	Racist Sexist Abusive in other ways

Personal Account

Name: Nicola Wilson
Date: 5 December 2005

Encourage groups to work together to comply with behaviour targets they have been set in relation to classroom discipline (2.2.2 2a)

I was working with RB's group in English. We were working on questions from a previous exam paper. Before I started to work with the group I reminded them that they must take it in turns to speak and that when one pupil is speaking they must listen.

Encourage and reinforce positive interactions between pupils (2.2.2 1ab)

Sometimes this group tends to be a bit chatty to say the least and they all speak at once. We were taking turns at reading the questions and talking about how we would answer the questions. The lads were behaving sensibly and listening to each other's suggestions and making positive comments about them. For example CK said that he thought RB's description was spot on. I praised the lads for working well together and staying on task.

Respond to conflict situations and incidents of anti-social behaviour in line with school policies and within the scope of your own responsibilities (2.2.2 5c)

Seek the assistance of appropriate staff where conflicts or anti-social behaviour occur that are outside of your role to resolve (2.2.2 6c)

RB at this point went on to read the next question. He had a few problems reading and started stammering at one point. DT from the other group was listening in and said: 'Come on you spastic – spit it out.' I immediately told DT that his language to RB was not appropriate and that I would be putting him on report. DT seemed shocked and quickly apologised. The teacher was aware of what was happening and asked DT to step outside.

Teacher's comments

Nicola worked well with the group. Nicola followed the school's procedure regarding abusive language. Abusive language is not tolerated at our school.

I certify that this is a true statement of what occurred.

Signed: M. Ames (Class Teacher) Date: 6 December 2005

Assessor's comments

A strong piece of evidence. Well done for marking in the performance indicators you have completed. This is a good example of responding to a situation that concerns pupils who are 'abusive in other ways'. However, as the teacher was monitoring what was happening and intervened you cannot really say that you sought her assistance. You will need to find an example for this indicator. (**Seek the assistance of appropriate staff where conflicts or anti-social behaviour occur that are outside of your role to resolve.**)

You could attach to this the report form you filled in regarding DT's abusive language. Again this could be cross-referenced to Unit 3.1 Contribute to the management of pupil behaviour.

While personal accounts provide good evidence – there are other sources of evidence, such as memos or incident report forms that you could include.

Signed: Terrie Cole

Terrie Cole
NVQ Assessor

The next week Nicola submitted a memo as evidence.

Memo:
Date: 12 December
To: Miss Talbot (Head of Year) cc Mr Simpson (Tutor 10A)

I have noticed that Dean Sanders of 10A has been extremely tired when I have been supporting him in class. At times he has found it very hard to keep his eyes open. This is most unlike Dean. I have asked why he is so tired, but he seems quite reluctant to talk about this.

Dear Nicola

Thanks for your note – I have now contacted Dean's home. His dad reports that his mother is in hospital and that Dean, as the oldest, now has a lot of responsibilities at home in caring for his 3 younger brothers. I am sure you will be supportive of Dean's situation.

M Talbot (Head of Year)

Assessor's comments

This evidence covers **recognising uncharacteristic behaviour patterns in the pupil and reporting these promptly to the relevant people, member of senior management team, (2.2.1 6c)**. More importantly this shows the value of your observations. I am sure you will be supportive of Dean.

As I said, you do not always need to write personal accounts. The performance indicators are meant to reflect what you do in your everyday work life. Therefore memos and incident report forms are good sources of evidence.

However remember confidentiality – remember to block names out on school records.

On a technical point, for memos to be used as evidence, it is important that the person who receives the memo signs them to state that they have indeed got the message. In this case the Head of Year responded to you on your original memo.

Signed: Terrie Cole

Terrie Cole
NVQ Assessor

Chapter 4

Unit 2.3 Provide support for learning activities

In this unit there are two elements:

2.3.1 Support the teacher in the planning and evaluation of learning activities
2.3.2 Support the delivery of learning activities

KNOWLEDGE BASE

2.3.1 Support the teacher in the planning and evaluation of learning activities

Objectives of the learning activities

The day-to-day life of a school can seem incredibly busy and even chaotic at times. But in order for schools to function they rely on careful and detailed planning. These plans are not made in isolation but will follow a **scheme of work** as detailed in the **National Curriculum**.

From the scheme of work the teacher will write up plans that would cover what the class will do during a term or half term. From these long-term plans, weekly and daily plans are drawn up. Some pupils will need to have their work differentiated, that is adapted to their ability level; this will include pupils who have individual learning targets as identified on IEPs.

In a day a pupil will participate in a variety of learning activities, such as maths, science, English and PE, as specified on the daily plan and each of these activities will have learning objectives or targets. See Appendix for examples of plans.

While it is useful for the TA and teacher to discuss the weekly plans in advance, it is essential that when working with an individual or a group the TA knows the learning objectives for that session.

The relationship between your own role and the role of the teacher within the learning environment

Planning and evaluation are important parts of teaching. In a sense teaching can be seen as a cycle and TAs will have a vital role to play in this cycle.

The teacher plans the lesson

- The teacher may show the TA weekly plans and ask for the TA's comments and suggestions.

- An important part of planning a lesson is stating what the learning objectives are. The teacher will inform the TA of the learning objectives.

The teacher and TA deliver the lesson

- During the delivery of the lesson the TA and the teacher may ask for feedback from the pupils regarding their understanding.
- Sometimes it is necessary to think on your feet and adapt or modify the lesson if some pupils are struggling.

The teacher and TA will evaluate the lesson

- Evaluation will include feedback on whether the pupils achieved the learning objectives or outcomes.
- Evaluation will also include comments on what went well with the lesson and what areas could be improved for next time.
- Evaluation will also include personal reflections regarding how you could improve on the way in which you supported the session.
- All these comments will be fed into future plans.

The teacher will plan the next day's lesson

- On the basis of previous evaluation the teacher will revise or adapt the lesson plan as necessary. In this sense we can see planning, delivering/teaching and evaluation as a never-ending cycle.

Formative and summative assessment

Assessment is part of evaluation. Assessment is important as it establishes what the pupil has learned and what still needs to be learnt. Assessment is an ongoing process. There are two types of assessment: summative assessment and formative assessment. Summative assessment records what the pupil knows at a certain point in time.

Examples of summative assessment are various types of tests. These tests could include:

- national tests, for example, SATs
- end of term tests
- commercially produced tests.

TAs may be involved in administering, marking and recording the results of the tests.

Formative assessment refers to continuous assessment that is carried out on a regular basis. Examples of formative assessment could be

- comments made in reading diaries
- marks and comments made in pupils' books.

TAs will be involved in formative assessment.

Formative assessment also involves the pupils' participation in evaluating how well they think they are doing. In recent years emphasis has been placed on **Assessment for Learning.**

Assessment for Learning involves evaluating the lesson as it is progressing and involves the pupils in evaluation. This means asking the pupil as they go along – 'How is it going?' or 'Do we understand this?'

In order for the pupils to make comments on their learning they first have to know what it is that they have to learn. Often teachers will write aims or learning objectives on the board. Some schools will use systems such as WALT (What are the lesson targets) or WILF (What I'm looking for).

In asking pupils how is it going some schools may use a traffic light system where pupils will hold up:

- a green card for 'I understand'
- a yellow card for 'Some things I understand and others I don't'
- a red card for 'I don't understand –I'm confused'.

Other schools will use a thumbs up, thumbs down system.

The advantage of using these systems is that it gives you information on which pupils understand the lesson. If there are pupils who don't understand it is important for the TA to modify their approach.

In Assessment for Learning the pupils are also encouraged to review their work and identify what they need to learn next. A TA can help the pupil do this.

As a TA it is also useful to know the **attainment levels** that the pupils should be working towards. Your teacher will have detailed knowledge of this.

Your role and responsibilities for supporting pupils' learning and the implications of this for the sort of support you can provide

and

Your experience and expertise in relation to supporting learning activities and how this relates to the planned activities

It is the responsibility of the teacher to both plan and evaluate the learning activities.

It is the role of the TA to assist the teacher in this task.

Age related expectations

Age (years)	*Class*	*Key Stage*	*Expected attainment levels for the majority of pupils*
4–5	Reception	Early Years **Foundation Stage**	
5–6	Year 1	Key Stage 1	
6–7	Year 2		SATs Level 2b
7–8	Year 3	Key Stage 2	
8–9	Year 4		
9–10	Year 5		
10–11	Year 6		SATs Level 4b
11–12	Year 7	Key Stage 3	
12–13	Year 8		
13–14	Year 9		SATs Level 5–6
14–15	Year 10	Key Stage 4	
15–16	Year 11		GCSE 5 A–C grades

Support TA can provide	*Examples of TAs using experience and expertise*	*How teachers can use TAs' experience*
TAs can offer suggestions as to the type of support they can provide to the planned activities.	'The class was to discuss World War II. I told the teacher that I had some interesting books and some old photographs my Nan took during the war that I could bring in.'	If teachers know the skills you have to offer, they can use your skills to enhance the quality of the lesson.
	'I have attended adult education classes in cake decoration. I told the teacher I would be happy to help the class decorate their Christmas Cakes.'	
TAs can point out any difficulties they see in the proposed plans.	'I mentioned to the teacher that I didn't think that pupil could cope with that work.'	Teachers value your comments regarding pupils.
	'I thought that the pupil would find working in the corridor outside the classroom too disruptive as they would be distracted by all the comings and goings.'	
	'If I am to help the pupils with ICT skills – I could benefit from some additional training myself.'	Teachers need to know what skills you need further training in, so that you can better support the pupils.
TAs can make sure that they are prepared for their contribution to the lesson.	'In a secondary school – I always make a point of trying to get to the class before the pupils so I can have a quick word with the teacher before the class starts.'	
	'I always make sure I have a supply of pens and pencils in case any of the pupils have forgotten their material.'	

After the lesson is over, it is important that TAs offer feedback to the teacher.	'I always make a point of telling the teacher who has achieved the learning objectives and who would require additional work on that area.'	Teachers need this information to plan future sessions.
	'I can offer feedback on the materials used.'	
	'If we have run out of certain materials. For example at Christmas time the pupils went mad on the red and green paint and we simply ran out. I informed the teacher and she was able to inform the bursar to place another order.'	Running out of required material is one problem that can be easily avoided.
	'I can offer feedback on my contribution to the activity.' 'Most of the time I feel that I am able to help the pupils understand what is required of them. However on some occasions, with some pupils, I feel that I am just not getting through. When I discuss this with the teacher, they often give me suggestions for what I can do to help the pupils understand.'	Supporting learning involves teamwork. If you are having difficulties a teacher can offer valuable advice so that you can support the pupils more effectively.
Provide the teacher with relevant information. This information is needed for teachers' records and reports.	'Part of my role is to hear the pupils read and to record this information in their reading diaries. From my comments the teacher can get a sense of how the pupil is progressing.'	Supporting learning is teamwork.
	'I am responsible for recording the information from the pupils' end of term tests.'	

How to give feedback in a constructive manner and in a way that ensures that working relationships are maintained

Constructive feedback involves giving both positive comments and helpful suggestions but in a manner that is perceived as helpful. Consideration is needed in doing this as helpful suggestions, if not carefully phrased, might be interpreted as put-downs or as criticisms. As a TA you will need to give constructive feedback to the other teaching professionals you work with.

Consider how you would comment on the following situations.

Situation	*Possible reply*
Mr Telford in the Maths class is having difficulties in controlling the class. You notice that though he threatens to give the pupils detentions he never does. Mr Telford remarks to you that the class is still out of control.	
Amy, a Year 2 pupil, has asked the supply teacher if she can sit next to her best friend. The supply teacher has agreed – but you know that the regular teacher never allows this and that Amy and her best friend sitting together is a recipe for disaster.	

2.3.2 Support the delivery of learning activities

Basic principles underlying pupil development and learning

Refer to diagram on page 58.

Matching teaching style to learning styles

Learning styles refers to the preferred manner in which an individual would choose to learn. There are many measures of learning styles. One of the most commonly used measures of learning styles divides learners into visual, auditory and kinaesthetic learners (see Figure 4.1).

Learning style	*Preferred learning activities*
Auditory	This individual remembers more if information to be learnt is presented verbally. This individual learns by having someone explain to them what they have to do. This individual will often revise for a test by reading out loud.
Visual	Visual learners need to see things in order to learn. Visual learners like to see someone else do an activity first. Visual learners take in information best by watching videos, studying maps, diagrams and pictures.
Kinaesthetic	These learners need to be physically involved in an activity in order to learn. These learners are very much hands on.

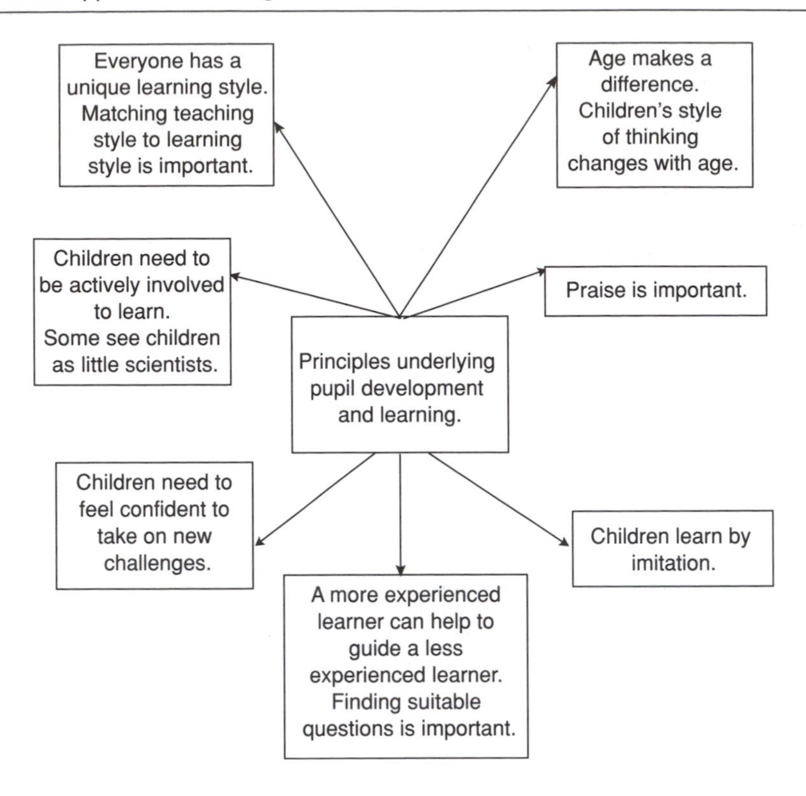

Figure 4.1 Learning style super heroes

Strategies to use for supporting pupils' learning

It is helpful to teach pupils in their preferred learning style. This is especially true with pupils who are struggling. Some schools are now giving pupils various questionnaires to measure their learning styles. If your school is doing this, then as a TA you can take advantage of this information. However, if you don't have this information you can watch how pupils learn and notice how they learn best.

With knowledge of a pupil's preferred learning style you can vary your approach. For example use visual approach for a visual learner.

As one TA comments:

> I was working with Sam helping him with a worksheet on maths coordinates. He was finding this very difficult to understand. I knew that Sam was a visual learner, so I quickly drew a treasure map with clues pointing to the location of the treasure. The clues were in the form of coordinates. Sam found this really interesting and quickly grasped the ideas of coordinates.

Although it is useful to adapt your style to the learning style of a pupil, it is also true that all pupils will benefit from information being presented in a variety of styles. Though individuals will have their preferred learning style it is also important to be able to learn in a variety of ways.

Age makes a difference

Theorists, such as Jean Piaget (1970), state that children's thinking changes with time. Piaget states that children go through stages reflecting their thinking abilities or cognitive development. The precise age when a child will go onto the next stage will vary from child to child. However, all children will go through all stages in the same order.

Stage	*Age*
Sensori-motor	0–2
Pre-operational	2–7
Concrete operational	7–11
Formal operational	11+

When a child first starts school Piaget would describe children as pre-operational thinkers. This stage lasts from 2 years to 7 years. Children within this age group are learning at an incredible rate. However, Piaget states that their learning is limited by egocentrism and the failure to conserve.

Children between the ages of 2 and 7 are egocentric

Egocentrism refers to the difficulty in seeing the world from another's point of view. The classic test for egocentrism is known as the 'Three Mountains Test' (Figure 4.2). Here a child is presented with a model of three mountains, one with snow on the top, one with a cross on the top and one with a cabin on the top. The child is then shown a range of pictures of this model. The child has to choose the picture showing the view that they see. This the child can do.

Figure 4.2 The 'Three Mountains Test'

Then the test gets more complicated. The child is shown a doll and the doll is placed at a point around the model of the three mountains. Then the child is asked to select the picture that the doll sees from where the doll is sitting. Often the child will select the picture that they can see.

From this test Piaget concluded that a young child tends to think that others see the world as they do. It is not till a child is 8 or 9 that they will realise that others will have their own viewpoint on the world and correctly select the picture that the doll can see.

Strategies to use for supporting pupils' learning: how TAs can use this knowledge in the classroom

Though this Three Mountains Test seems obscure, the fact that a child has difficulties appreciating another's viewpoint has implications for those working with children in this age group. The ability to see the world from another's viewpoint is related to the ability of empathy, where a child can imagine what another child would be feeling.

Teaching assistants can encourage children to think about how other children think and feel.

Children between the ages of 2 and 7 have difficulties conserving

Piaget also said that this pre-operational stage was dominated by the inability to conserve. Conservation, or to conserve, requires an individual to hold two apparently conflicting ideas in their mind at the same time. Again this idea seems complex.

Let's take an example of conservation of liquid. Two children aged 4 and 8 are given one can of drink to share. For the children involved it would be very important that each has the same amount.

As a TA you select two identical cups, two short, clear and wide cups and very carefully measure the same amount of liquid into each cup.

At this point after some consideration the children will probably agree that there is the same amount of drink in each and that this is fair.

However, if at that point you realise that one of the cups is chipped and pour the amount into a different shaped cup, let's say a clear tall thin cup, you may have problems with convincing the younger child that there is the same amount in this cup.

A younger child of 4 might say that this is no longer fair as the tall thin cup has more liquid. It looks like it has more therefore it has more.

An older child of 8 might reason that, as one cup is short and fat, the other cup is tall and thin. An older child will realise that though the cups holding the drink look different, actually they are holding the same amount of liquid.

This skill of logic, involving holding two apparently conflicting views in your mind, is the ability to conserve (see Figure 4.3).

Children of 7–11 are concrete thinkers

Children can do more complex operations such as multiplication and division and fractions but can do only these calculations on objects that actually exist, hence the word concrete. For example three-quarters of 12 can be calculated but '¾ *of x*' does not make sense.

Figure 4.3 Conservation skills

Children of 11 plus move into the stage of formal operations

Piaget felt that children do not gain the ability to think abstractly until they reach the final stage of formal operations. This stage applies to children of the ages of 11 and over. It is for this reason that algebra is not taught to children until they are this age.

Strategies to use for supporting pupils' learning: how TAs can use this knowledge in the classroom

TAs can help pupils develop skills in logic by encouraging pupils to experiment and discover things for themselves. Pupils learn new information more easily if you can give them specific examples of real-life experiences that they can relate the new information to. Pupils benefit from using real apparatus.

If we remember, Piaget said that though children will go through all the stages in the same order the age with which they can enter the next stage will vary from child to child.

Therefore, though the curriculum in secondary school assumes that older children can think more abstractly, some pupils who are struggling will not have this skill and will benefit from being given specific examples related to real-life objects. Though they are older Piaget might say that they are still thinking at a less advanced level.

To learn children need to be actively involved

Piaget felt that a child's thinking ability was influenced by the age of the child and the interaction the child has with their environment.

Certain topics cannot be taught to a child until the child is biologically or mentally ready to understand these concepts. Piaget talks about maturational readiness. If a child in Reception is having difficulties learning to read perhaps it is because they are just not ready and that when they are ready they will learn.

However, to learn a child needs to be actively involved in the learning process. Piaget sees children as little scientists and that they need to discover knowledge for themselves. Piaget believed that when we learn information we store this information in the form of schemas. Schemas are units of mental thought. Schemas are developed through the process of assimilation and accommodation.

Assimilation involves taking in new information and filing this information into an existing schema.

Accommodation is involved in the creation of new schemas or new ways of thinking. Accommodation is more complex. To create a schema or unit of new knowledge the individual first has to realise that:

- there is a gap in their understanding
- others are seeing things differently
- they are wrong and that they need to think in a different way.

Piaget called the state of being aware that there was a gap in understanding, cognitive disequilibrium. Piaget said that being in a state of cognitive disequilibrium was unpleasant but that it was a motivating force to learn new information.

Figure 4.4 The perils of discovery learning

In a sense, what Piaget is saying is that to learn new information you first have to realise that there is something you don't understand (see Figure 4.4).

Strategies to use for supporting pupils' learning: how TAs can use this knowledge in the classroom

TAs can help pupils to realise that getting stuck and not understanding is an important part of the learning process. Remember pupils need to discover things for themselves. TAs can create situations or asks questions so that children can realise for themselves that there are things that they don't understand.

A more experienced learner can help to guide a less experienced learner

While Piaget stated that children learn new information through the process of discovery, Vygotsky (1986), another theorist, argued that children learn by being guided by a more experienced learner. This experienced learner could be the teacher, the TA or a more able pupil. One of Vygotsky's key ideas was the Zone of Proximal Development. The Zone of Proximal Development states that what a pupil can do with assistance or help today they could do by themselves in time.

Of course to guide a pupil in learning is easier said that done. Successful guidance involves communicating knowledge to the pupil in a way that they can understand. Finding suitable questions is important.

Strategies to use for supporting pupils' learning: how TAs can use this knowledge in the classroom

Often it is the TAs who work with pupils who find learning difficult. Often a TA will need to explain something several times and perhaps in several different ways before the pupil shows some understanding.

As pupils can learn from more experienced learners, TAs can encourage more able pupils to help pupils who are struggling. These pupils may be able to find the right words to explain that concept the pupil finds so difficult to understand.

As pupils can learn from each other it is helpful in group situations to encourage children not only to share the answers, but also to share how they came to that answer. It is also important to communicate to the pupils that there are sometimes many ways to solve a problem.

Children need to feel confident to take on new challenges: praise is important

Here we see that how children feel about themselves influences their ability to learn. In a sense we are talking about self-esteem. Those individuals with high self-esteem are prepared to take on new challenges. Individuals with high self-esteem are prepared to make mistakes and to learn from their mistakes.

As we have said before, getting stuck, not knowing the answer, is the first step in building new ways of understanding. Unfortunately some pupils are afraid of making mistakes and would rather not do the work than to do the work and fail.

Strategies to use for supporting pupils' learning

As a TA you will need to encourage pupils to take on new learning challenges and help them to deal with setbacks in a positive manner. As a TA you will need to praise the pupil. Praise should be given for the effort that they have put into the task rather than whether they got the question right or wrong.

Children learn by imitation

As we have mentioned previously some individuals have a visual learning style, that is they learn best by watching and imitating. To an extent all children learn by this process.

If learning was just about watching what others do and imitating what they do – learning would be easy. But what makes imitation difficult is knowing what to pay attention to and being able to copy that behaviour when it comes to your turn.

We have all had experiences when someone has said: 'Right this is easy, watch what I do and then you do it next.' However, whether they are demonstrating how to mend a photocopier, how to parallel park or how to make a soufflé it is not quite that easy. Often the task is difficult to imitate because there are many steps involved and each of these steps involves practice.

As a TA when you are asking a child to watch what you are doing and then imitate the task it is important that:

- you make sure the pupil is paying attention
- you break the task into small steps
- you praise effort and encourage the pupil to practise the steps on their own.

The sorts of problems that might occur when supporting learning activities with individuals and groups

What is presented in the table here are the sort of problems that might occur when supporting learning activities with individuals and groups. Throughout this chapter we have talked about various ways to support and encourage learning. Using the strategies and tips from this chapter and other chapters, fill in the table. To help you get started a few suggestions have been given.

Checklist

- ✔ When working with an individual or group, I know the learning objectives for that session.
- ✔ I give feedback in a constructive manner.
- ✔ I match teaching style to learning style.
- ✔ I encourage the pupils to be actively involved.
- ✔ I give lots of praise.

Activity: Problems that might occur in supporting learning

Problems that might occur in supporting learning	*Possible explanations*	*Strategies that can be used to support learning*
Pupils may find the task too difficult.	Possibly the student is not ready (maturation readiness)	
Pupils may not understand the task.	Possibly not teaching to learning style	
Pupils may say they are bored and they don't want to do the task.	Perhaps pupils need to be more involved	Use discovery learning
One pupil may not want to join in.		
Pupils may not be paying attention.		
A pupil may say that they are stupid and that they cannot do a task.		
Pupils might be distracted by other activities.		
They might persistently ask when it is time for break or when it is time for lunch.		
Even if the group is a middle or lower set – there still may be a range of abilities.		
One pupil always wants to dominate the group.		
The pupil who likes to criticise other pupils.		
The needy pupil.		
Having several needy pupils fighting for your attention.		
When playing a game the pupil who always wants to go first.		
When playing a game the pupil who finds it hard to lose.		

MEETING PERFORMANCE INDICATORS

2.3.1 Support the teacher in the planning and evaluation of learning activities

Setting the scene

At college Miranda's tutor suggests that all the NVQ 2 candidates plan a short session that they will deliver to a small group of pupils. Miranda's tutor states that they will need to plan the session with the teacher, ask the teacher to observe them conducting the session and have the teacher write up what they observe.

As Miranda's teacher knows she is enrolled on an NVQ 2 teaching assistants course, she arranges the time to talk to Miranda about the session and arranges suitable cover so she can observe Miranda at work.

Miranda, when planning the session, looks at some of the performance indicators for this unit.

Unit 2.3.1 Support the teacher in the planning and evaluation of learning activities

Performance indicators	*Scope*
(1) Offer constructive and timely suggestions as to the support you can provide to a planned activity.	(a) Relating to a single lesson (b) Relating to activities spanning several lessons
(2) Give constructive information on any difficulties you can identify with your ability to provide the support needed.	(a) Inadequate time (b) Need or additional expertise and/or development
(3) Make sure you are adequately prepared for your contribution to the learning activity.	
(4) Offer constructive feedback on the activity in discussion with the teacher.	(a) On the pupils' response to it (b) On the materials used (c) On your contribution to supporting the activity
(5) Share comments with the teacher at an appropriate time and place, and in a way that maintains effective working relationships.	
(6) Provide relevant information to contribute to the teacher's records and reports.	

Miranda discusses the session with the teacher and writes a plan to show her assessor.

Name: Miranda Appleton

Session Plan
Activity: Comprehension
Date: 6 February 2006
Number in group: 4
Age: Reception

Description of the group

I will be working with the lower ability group.
James and Matthew have difficulty paying attention.
Charlotte and Angie are very shy and need encouragement to participate in group discussions.

Aim of activity

Encourage pupils to contribute to group discussions.
To be able to answer questions regarding the story.
Draw a picture about the story and describe the picture.

Materials

The book we were to read was a story about a group of teddy bears that went on a picnic in the rain.

Methods to be used

Read story to children.
Ask children questions about the story. For example what clothes do you wear when it is raining? What clothes were the teddy bears wearing?
Role-play – getting ready to go out for a rainy day picnic.
Ask children to draw picture of a rainy day picnic and discuss their picture with the group.

Key points to be developed

Have children think about the book and discuss the weather and what types of clothes they would wear for a rainy day.

Expected outcomes

Hope that all the pupils are able to answer questions relating to the story.

However, Miranda has a few concerns about this unit and writes a note to her assessor.

> Dear Terrie
>
> I have written a plan as you asked. My teacher was very supportive and talked this through with me and was willing to observe me conducting a short session. However I don't see how I am going to meet the indicators where I 'offer constructive and timely suggestions as to the support you can provide and give constructive information on any difficulties'.
>
> I really don't see how I am going to do this! My role is to support the teacher and not to tell the teacher what to do – that is not my place!
>
> xxx
>
> Miranda

The next day Miranda conducts her session. Miranda feels that the session went really well and is surprised at why she felt so worried about it in the first place.

Miranda brings in her evidence to college.

Record of Observation/Witness Statement

Name: Miranda Appleton
Name of observer: Mrs Higglesmith

When Miranda came to me with the request that I could observe her with a small group we discussed the aims and lesson objectives for that day.

I discussed how I would like Miranda to work with the Blue Group for a brief 15-minute session. Several of the children in this group have difficulties with maintaining attention and are somewhat reluctant to participate. When I showed Miranda the story she was to read, Miranda suggested that she could bring in some props, various teddy bears, rain boots and umbrellas. Miranda suggested that to encourage the pupils to be involved in the activity they act out the book as they go along. I told Miranda that I thought this was a great idea. Miranda then noted that if they were to do this that they might disrupt other pupils working in the class and that 15 minutes might not be long enough. We agreed that Miranda's group would go to the resource centre and that they would be given an extra five minutes. I also mentioned to Miranda that the HLTA would cover the class for myself when I was observing Miranda.

In observing Miranda, I noted that:

- Before commencing the story Miranda reminded the pupils of how they were to behave during the session.

- Miranda pitched the story correctly to the level of the children.
- Miranda was very good at engaging the children in the activity. Miranda encouraged the more shy members of the group to participate and divided her attention well between all members of the group. Miranda used constant praise to help the pupils stay on task.
- At the end of the session she had each pupil stand up and describe their picture of a rainy day. After each pupil presented their picture she and the entire group gave the pupil a round of applause.

A very effective session where all learning objectives were met. A lovely use of role-play. I was very impressed with the work Miranda had put into the session and the amount of props she had collected at home.

Signature: Mrs Higglesmith Class Teacher
Date: 10 February 2006

Evidence covered: 2.3.1 la, 2a, 3, 5
2.3.2 lb 3, 5

Assessor's comments

This is very strong evidence for this unit. As you can see I have written at the end of the teacher's witness statement what performance indicators you have met. I know you were worried about finding evidence for **giving constructive suggestions** but the witness statement clearly illustrates that you did this: 'by suggesting a role play activity and the types of props you could bring in', and 'noting that 15 minutes was not long enough for the activity'.

I think you were reading too much into **constructive and timely suggestions** – in fact you probably make suggestions like this all the time. Remember teachers need and value your comments!

There are still a number of performance indicators to complete for this unit on offering constructive feedback regarding the activity and providing relevant information to contribute to the teacher's records.

Here you could include a written account of the feedback you gave the teacher, including any forms or recording sheets you have filled in. You might be able to cross reference to the unit on literacy and numeracy.

Well done!

Signed: Terrie Cole

Terrie Cole
NVQ Assessor

Later that week at college Miranda tells the others about how she has got on and that really it was quite easy. Miranda reports that her teacher always discusses the weekly lesson plans with her and that she was only too willing to help her with this task.

The other TAs were not quite so enthusiastic about the task and expressed their concerns to the college tutor.

Nicola: It is easy for TAs in primary schools to do this task – but it is not that easy for a TA in a secondary school. Sometimes in a secondary school you don't know what you will be doing until you get into class and the teacher tells the group. Weekly lesson plans, daily lesson plans – I never see them. No, actually the only time I saw them was when Ofsted came in. Often I don't work with groups. I work supporting pupils who are often seated at various places in the room. The teacher is so busy – there is no way they will be able to observe me for 20 minutes. Who will look after the rest of the class?

Sam: It is the same with us volunteers. Often I don't know what we are doing for the day. When the teacher explains the work to the class I have to listen very carefully otherwise I would not know what I was supposed to be doing! As for the teacher observing me –well again he is so busy.

College tutor: When you signed up for this course you needed the school's support to do so and this is where they need to support you.

Perhaps in a secondary school you could ask to spend some time working in a unit with pupils who are receiving extra support in regard to literacy and numeracy.

Perhaps you could ask the secondary teacher if you could have all the pupils you are working with in the class to sit together.

Also many schools will have appraisal systems operating for teaching assistants and this observation can be used as part of your appraisal.

As for seeing weekly lesson plans mention to your teacher or SENCO that you would really benefit from seeing them and that as part of your course you do need to see them. If there are any problems with this mention this to your assessor and they will have a word with your teacher.

Chapter 5

Unit 2.4 Provide effective support for your colleagues

In this unit there are two elements:

2.4.1 Maintain working relationships with colleagues
2.4.2 Develop your effectiveness in a support role

KNOWLEDGE BASE

2.4.1 Maintain working relationships with colleagues

Working together

It has been said that no man is an island. While this is true for any individual it is especially true for those working in a school. For a school to run smoothly teamwork is essential. Teamwork involves the elements illustrated in the diagram.

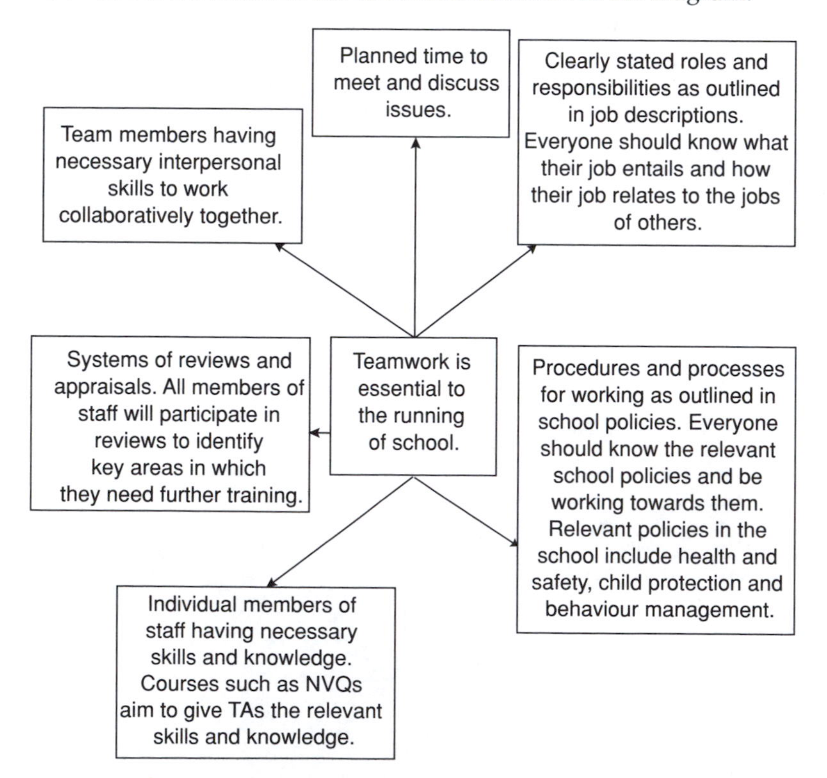

Your role and responsibilities and how they relate to the role of colleagues with whom you work

Every member of staff will have a job description. This job description will outline your responsibilities within the school. In addition many schools nowadays rely on volunteers coming in on a regular basis. If you are working within a school on a volunteer basis there should be a designated member of staff to whom you are responsible. Further some schools will have a job description for volunteers.

A summary of a typical job description for a primary teaching assistant could look like this. Many job descriptions will include more details than the one mentioned in the box below.

Anywhere Primary

Job title:	Teaching assistant.
Job purpose:	To ensure, in collaboration with other teaching professionals, that the aims and objectives of the school are achieved through the delivery of the National Curriculum and the provision of other activities which promote optimum child development.
Responsible to:	Initially to class teacher and ultimately to head teacher/deputy head teacher/SENCO.
Accountable for:	Providing classroom, small group and individual support as required.

Key accountabilities

1. To assist with the organisation of the classroom and preparation of activities.
2. To observe pupil behaviour and to share in the responsibility for the well-being and discipline of all pupils.
3. To assist in the teaching and learning process as required.
4. To work in cooperation with other teaching professionals to ensure that equal opportunities and equal access to the curriculum exists for all pupils across all age groups.

A summary of a typical job description for a secondary teaching assistant could look like the one shown in the box below.

Wherever Secondary

Job title:	Teaching assistant.
Job purpose:	To support teachers and students in the classroom. To support students in examinations. To help with clerical work in the department.
Accountable to:	SENCO.

Key accountabilities

1. To support pupils in the classroom.
2. To read texts and scribe responses for designated pupils as appropriate.
3. To help pupils plan and organise their work.
4. To explain work to pupils as necessary.
5. To give social and emotional support to all pupils and in doing so help to build positive self-esteem.
6. To work with individuals, groups or classes as required.
7. To assist teachers with the differentiation of work.
8. To keep necessary records as required.
9. To support designated pupils in exam settings as required.
10. To help with clerical work in the preparation, photocopying and organising of materials as required.
11. To communicate effectively with pupils and all members of staff.

Teaching assistants do not work in isolation. An effective school relies on teamwork. The table on pages 75–6 shows a list of 'Who's who' in a school.

Basic principles underlying effective communication, interpersonal and collaborative skills

Communication and interpersonal skills involve **active listening**.

Active listening involves being able to acknowledge your own feelings and being aware of how they might influence your reactions to others

Teaching assistant: Sometimes I can have a very stressful morning. I am on my own with three children and it takes a lot of work to get them ready for school, their lunch boxes prepared and the youngest dropped off at my mother's before I can get to school. If I have had a particularly difficult morning I can get quite snappy and abrupt especially with the new TA who has just started helping out in the class. I know that I need to not take things out or lose my patience with other members of staff.

Active listening means really listening to what the other person has to say

Teaching assistant: I find accepting criticism difficult. I know that sometimes they are just trying to give me suggestions about how to do things better next time. But it is like when I hear them say 'You should have done that' that I just shut down and get angry and upset. In fact sometimes I am so upset I really don't hear what they have to say. I know I have to learn to take comments on my work as suggestions rather than criticisms.

Position	*Duties*	*Examples of how a TA interacts with these professionals*
Governors	The governors with the head teacher make the final decisions about how the school is run. The governors will deal with issues relating to finance, curriculum and special needs. The governors will include members of the community, parents, teachers and representatives from the local authority.	The governors are there to give assistance and advice as required. As a TA you might meet one of the governors when they visit the school. Some TAs themselves are governors and gain a useful insight on the school from this role.
Head teacher	The head teacher is responsible for managing all aspects of the school. The head teacher needs to ensure that the curriculum is effectively taught and that the well-being of the pupils is ensured.	Head teachers are busy people, but they make time to listen to all those involved with the school.
Deputy head teacher	The deputy head teacher is second in command. The deputy is there to assist the head in managing the school and will take the responsibility for the school when the head is absent.	
SENCO	The Special Educational Needs Coordinator is responsible for all pupils registered as having special educational needs. The duties of the SENCO will involve monitoring pupils, writing, updating and reviewing IEPs.	SENCOs are very busy people. They also have a wealth of information regarding how to deal with pupils who face particular challenges. They will offer advice to teachers and teaching assistants on what strategies could be used with pupils who are having difficulties.
Secretarial and administration staff	These members of staff are responsible for greeting visitors, answering phone-calls, typing, sending out required correspondence and maintaining necessary records.	
Bursar	The bursar is in charge of the finances of the school.	The bursar will know how much money the school has to spend on training and continuing professional development.
Curriculum coordinators and subject managers	These are teachers who are given special areas of responsibility. In this case the teachers will be responsible for a certain subject or curriculum area. In primary school this could be Key Stage 2 Maths or it could be Head of Maths at a secondary level.	
Heads of year or key stage	These are teachers who are given the responsibility of meeting the pastoral needs of pupils within a year group or key stage.	At a secondary level if a pupil you are working with starts behaving in an uncharacteristic manner, the Head of Year is a good person to talk to. The Head of Year may be able to talk to the pupil's family to see if there are any issues going on that are affecting the pupil.

Classroom teachers	Each teacher will have responsibility for planning, preparing, delivering and evaluating the learning for the classes which they support.	As a TA most of your work will be with the class teacher to which you are assigned.
Senior teaching assistants or HLTAs	In some schools there are a large number of TAs. In some schools there may be one senior TA who has responsibility for organising the work of all the TAs within the school. Some TAs will have gained the status of HLTAs and will be given extra responsibilities.	Senior TAs or HLTAs can offer valuable advice and training to TAs who are just starting out.
Teaching assistants	Teaching assistants can be assigned to work with a specific class or assigned to work with a specific pupil with special educational needs. In secondary schools TAs might be assigned to work with a specific year group supporting those pupils within the year group who are on the SEN Register. Some TAs at secondary school are assigned to work within departments.	The advice, encouragement and support you get from your fellow TAs is invaluable.
Volunteer TAs	Volunteer TAs are dedicated individuals, who are interested in education and are giving up their free time to help teachers to effectively manage their classroom.	Often volunteer TAs go on to full or part-time employment within a school.
School nurse	This member of staff is responsible for dealing with minor accidents, making decisions regarding when to call for further medical assistance and for administering necessary medication.	As a TA you will need to know who these individuals are.
First aiders	These are members of staff who have taken courses in 'first aid' and know what to do in the event of medical emergencies.	
Cleaning staff	These members of staff start to work before other staff arrive for the day or when the teaching staff prepare to go home. They ensure that the working environment of the school is in a clean state.	
Site security	These members of staff are often found in large schools. These staff members are there to ensure the premises are safe from unwanted intruders. These staff will often have the duty of ensuring that the buildings are secure at the end of a teaching day.	
Caretaker	This member of staff is responsible for the maintenance of the school building.	
Meal-time supervisors	These individuals are responsible for setting up the dining hall for many hungry pupils. They are responsible for ensuring appropriate behaviour is maintained during the lunch hours and they are responsible for clearing up afterwards.	Some TAs may also work as meal-time supervisors.

Active listening means communicating to the other person that you value and respect them

Teaching assistant: It is important when working together to find something good to say about a person's work and not to take them for granted. After a very difficult day in the class I mentioned to the teacher that though the class was still difficult that there was an improvement and that it was very much down to her hard work with the group. The teacher was very touched and thankful for my comments.

Good communication skills involve knowing how to say difficult things in a positive manner

Teaching assistant: I always try to do this with pupils who are struggling – but it is more difficult with other staff members. Sometimes the teacher says to me after the class –that went well – didn't it. However sometimes the session did not go well at all – sometimes to be honest I could say it was a disaster – but what can I say to the teacher? In a sense I know that she is looking to me for reassurance and I am not sure if it is my place to criticise or make judgements.

Teaching assistant: I find the same difficulties – however the teacher I work with welcomes my suggestions and I always start by telling him what I thought went well with the session.

Good communication skills involve dealing with issues before they become problems

Teaching assistant: I always find it helpful in the long run to be open about any problems. Last year at my school it was always the same TA who was chosen to go to any training days. Rather than just talk about this behind her back we decided to raise the issue of training at our next TA meeting. Well it was good that we talked about it. As it turns out the TA who was going on all those training days was due to start working with a pupil with complex special needs. The head teacher since that meeting has put all of the TAs down on a rota for training.

Good communication skills involve realising and valuing the contribution you can make towards the successful running of the school

Teaching assistant: When I first started working at the school I felt very overwhelmed and was very anxious about talking to teachers. Now I feel more confident about putting my ideas forward, not only to the teacher, but sometimes I will make suggestions in our staff and TA meetings.

Good teamwork involves knowing how to relate to each other on a professional basis

Teaching assistant: I see some of the staff members on a social basis and though we are very much first name basis in the pub – at school I always will address members of staff by their titles and treat them with respect and courtesy. I know that the children will be watching how we, the staff, treat each other and that the way we treat each other should be an example of how they, the pupils, should try to get on with each other.

Teaching assistant: An important part of your job involves maintaining confidentiality. There are some things in the school that are made known on a 'need to know' basis. This means that there are some things that you will be told in confidence and some details which while you can discuss at school do not get discussed once you leave the school.

The meeting and consultation structure within the school

In schools there are always meetings.

- *Planning meetings:* teachers, head teachers, subject coordinators will be involved with planning how the school will deliver the curriculum.
- *Meetings regarding individual pupils:* teachers, head teachers, SENCOs, members of outside agencies (for example speech and language therapist) parents and teaching assistants may be involved in meetings relating to IEPs.
- *Staff meetings:* all school staff may attend these meetings where specific issues relating to the whole school are discussed. Items on the agenda may include the upcoming Ofsted inspection, plans for future in-service training (INSET) days and where to go for the staff Christmas lunch.
- *Specific meetings:* there may be separate meetings for relevant members of staff (be they the senior management, governors, teaching assistants, teachers) to discuss issues specific to them. These meetings are held as the need arises. Some schools will have special forums for teaching assistants to meet and discuss issues relating to their work.

Lines of communication and methods of communication that apply within the school setting

In addition to meetings there are procedures whereby staff members can communicate with each other.

Watch the notice board

Often the notice board at school has a wealth of relevant information. Notes could include rotas for supervision at breaks, information on available courses and lists of pupils who have been currently excluded.

Memos, notes, filling in records and the like

Often if you wish to communicate with another member of staff, you can write them a note. This note might need to be written on a specially designed paper or possibly might need to be written in a specific book. For example, notifying the IT specialist that there is a problem with a particular computer requires filling in a specific report form. In some very large schools each member of staff will have their own pigeon hole where you can leave them information and likewise collect relevant information. In addition school staff will often have their own email accounts.

Informal discussions

Often it is at break, during lunch hour, before class begins for the day or at the end of the day that you will have a chance to talk to the teacher about lesson plans, what went well, how a pupil coped with a maths worksheet and possible ideas for future sessions. In many schools a specific time in the day will be put aside for you to meet with your teacher.

School policies and procedures for dealing with difficulties in working relationships and practices

All schools should have a Grievance Policy for all staff. This procedure will be used when a member of staff has a problem that cannot be resolved by any other means.

The governing body is responsible for establishing the Grievance Policy. This policy will include:

- the opportunity for an employee to put his or her own case
- the right for the employee to be represented by a fellow worker or a trade union official
- for the case to be considered fairly and impartially
- the right to a reasonable timetable
- for the absence of victimisation once the procedure is initiated
- for the opportunity for a grievance to be resolved as quickly as possible.

It is hoped that any problems that you have in school can be resolved without going through a grievance procedure.

Possible problems within a school could include:

- bullying by other members of staff
- sexual harassment
- unfair dismissal
- discrimination

Let's hope that as a TA you will never have any problems in this regard. But if any of these issues were to develop it is good to know that there is a procedure in place.

2.4.2 Develop your effectiveness in a support role

Appraisal systems in use within the employment context

In the changing world of education, teaching assistants need to constantly think about how they do their job and in what ways could they do their jobs better. One way of doing this is by having an official review with your teacher or SENCO on a regular basis. In some schools these reviews are called professional discussions and in other schools they are called appraisals.

An appraisal looks at the following elements:

- How you are progressing in your duties. What duties are you doing at the moment? Does your job description match what you are currently doing?
- The areas you feel confident in.
- The areas you find difficult.
- The areas you need further training in.

The outcome of an appraisal is that you set yourself targets that you would like to work towards for the upcoming year.

A clear example of the paperwork and thinking involved in this process will be given in the second part of this chapter.

Development opportunities available to you and how to access these

Things never stand still in the field of education.

> Teaching assistant: My school is now trying to become a dyslexia friendly school.
>
> Teaching assistant: With the introduction of PPA time – I am now required to work with whole classes.
>
> Teaching assistant: I have a new role within the school – working in the behavioural unit.

Teaching assistants, as valued members of the teaching workforce, will be given opportunities to develop necessary skills for their evolving role (see Figure 5.1).

Continuing professional development (CPD) is important for all teaching professionals.

The opportunities available to TAs include

- INSET or school-based training
- having a mentor within the school
- attending networks or support groups for teaching assistants
- enrolling on specific courses for teaching assistants.

Checklist

- ✔ I make time to talk to the teacher.
- ✔ I participate in a self-appraisal and a formal review/appraisal if possible.
- ✔ I know the relevant school policies.
- ✔ I use active listening skills.
- ✔ I take advantage of developmental opportunities that come my way.

Figure 5.1 TA training: mission impossible

MEETING PERFORMANCE INDICATORS

2.4.2 Develop your effectiveness in a support role

Setting the scene

Part of Miranda's job involved her having an appraisal with her SENCO. Miranda stated that when she first heard about this she was a bit anxious. However now that she has gone through the process she sees appraisals as an opportunity to have a really useful discussion with her teacher. As Miranda states: 'The appraisal has made me more aware of all the work that I have been doing in the school and has helped me focus on what I need to do to improve my practice.'

Her assessor at college stated that Miranda should include the documentation for her appraisal as evidence for Unit 2.4.2

Miranda looks at *some* of the performance indicators for this unit.

Unit 2.4.2 Develop your effectiveness in a support role

Performance indicators	*Scope*
(1) Maintain an up-to-date understanding of the requirements of your role and responsibilities.	
(2) Seek and take account of constructive feedback on your performance from competent others.	
(3) Take an active part in identifying and agreeing personal development objectives which are realistic, achievable, specific, measurable and time related.	
(4) Undertake agreed development actions conscientiously and within the required time-scale.	
(5) Make effective use of the development support available to you.	(a) Training days and activities (b) Materials (c) Mentors (d) Networks

Miranda presents her evidence to her assessor.

Self-appraisal form for TAs

Name: Miranda Appleton
Position: TA

What I feel have been the key tasks and responsibilities of my job in relation to:

- *supporting the school*
- *supporting the pupils*
- *supporting my colleagues*
- *supporting the curriculum*

My key task within the school is to assist the teacher and to support the pupils as required. This may be listening to individuals read, working with specific groups on social skills or helping the less able groups with work.

As I have been working in the school for almost a year, some of the new TAs come to me for suggestions. I am willing to help them as I remember how I felt when I first started working at the school.

Aspects of my work I'm most pleased with and why

I find working with the pupils most rewarding. I find it amazing how pupils that I have worked with develop and really come on with time.

Aspects of my work I would like to improve and why

Even though I have worked in the school for almost a year I still have problems in getting some pupils to listen to me.

Things preventing me working as effectively as I would like

Not being able to talk to the teacher as much as I would like to. Though we do have five to ten minutes put aside at the beginning of the day – I feel that this is just not enough.

Changes I feel would improve my effectiveness

Finishing my NVQ course will help me understand the relevant knowledge and skills that I need to have to be a TA.

I would benefit from training on how to use an interactive whiteboard and more training on how to use the computer packages at school.

Being able to meet with the teacher more would help.

My key aims for next year

Develop more confidence in dealing with behaviour.
To have training in regard to interactive whiteboards and computer packages.
To finish the NVQ 2 course.

Training I would like to have

Training in using interactive whiteboards and computer packages.

How I would like my career to develop

Eventually I would like to work towards an NVQ 3 and when my children get older I would like to go to the local university and enrol on a foundation degree.

Signed: M. Appleton (TA) Date 16 May 2006

Appraisal with teaching assistants

Name of TA:	Miranda Appleton
Name of appraiser:	M. Higglesmith (SENCO)
Date of current appraisal:	22 May 2006
Date of previous appraisal (where applicable):	N/A

Targets set at last appraisal (where applicable)	Outcomes
1 N/A started Sept. 2005	1
2	2
3	3

Achievements over the past year with regard to:

(i.e. what has gone well, what the TA is most pleased with)

Support for the pupil

Miranda relates well to all pupils.
Miranda listens to all the pupils read and has fed back to me regarding their progress. Her feedback is detailed and considered.
Miranda works well with pupils in small groups and helps them to reach their learning objectives. If needed Miranda can adapt the lesson to meet the pupils' needs.

Support for the teacher(s)

Miranda is very good at using her initiative. If something needs to be done, Miranda gets on with the task.

Support for the school

Miranda was very involved in preparation for the school's Christmas play and I am pleased that Miranda has volunteered to help organise the summer fete.

Type of training received (with dates)

Sept./05 – training on how to use EpiPen
Nov./05 – county training day

Summary of what was learnt

- Procedures for using EpiPen
- Input on numeracy and literacy curriculum

Impact on what the TA does

As we have pupils in school who require an EpiPen to be used in a medical emergency, Miranda feels confident that she could administer the medication if required. Miranda is now more confident in guided reading sessions.

Further considerations

Miranda has expressed interest in taking a first aid course.

Areas for development

(i.e. what may not have gone so well or what needs to be learnt/taken on board)

Support for pupils

As Miranda's children attend this school, Miranda already knew many of the children before she started to work in this class. At first some of the children always referred to her as Jimmy's mum and did not treat her with the same respect as they would have another member of staff. This has improved greatly with time. The longer Miranda is in the school the easier this will become. I do not feel behaviour management is now an issue, but Miranda has expressed interest on further input in this area.

Support for the teacher(s)

More training on ICT. With this training Miranda would be able to offer more assistance and guidance to the pupils.

Support for the school

I know Miranda stated that when she was in secondary school she played for the girls' hockey team. As we plan to start a team next year it would be great if Miranda could offer her support.

Career aspirations and possibilities

Finish NVQ 2
Progress to NVQ 3

Targets for the next year

1 First aid training
2 Training in ICT and interactive white boards
3 Attend further INSET on behaviour

Action to be taken

What action?	By whom?	By when?
First aid	SENCO to arrange	Gain qualification by July 06
Interactive whiteboard training	ICT coordinator	asap
Behaviour INSET days	SENCO	Spring 07

Date for next appraisal: June 2007

Signed: M. Higglesmith (appraiser)
TA: M. Appleton

Diary of training events (compiled by Miranda Appleton)

Date	*Event*	*Witness signature*	*Witness position*	*Evidence Unit 2.4.2*
20 Sept.	School nurse gives demonstration on how to use EpiPen. This is essential to know as we have one pupil within the school who would in an emergency need this medication. We were given the opportunity to practise administering this drug by using a dummy EpiPen on ourselves.	J. Harris	School nurse	5a
21 Oct.	INSET day on becoming a dyslexia friendly school. Over the course of the year we will have sessions on different ways of detecting dyslexia, developmental coordination disorder, attention deficit disorder and specific language impairment.	G. Talbot	Trainer	5a
28 Nov.	County training day for teaching assistants at professional development centre. At the day we had a chance to meet 60 other TAs from across the county. We had specific workshops on literacy, numeracy and the Higher Level Teaching Assistant qualification.	G. Taylor	County advisor	5d
30 Jan.	Training afternoon with TAs from neighbouring schools. In groups we talked about how we dealt with behavioural difficulties.	G. Taylor	County advisor	5cd
27 Feb.	Input at college. Lecturer from local university came to our college and gave presentation on Foundation degrees available to teaching assistants.	D. Wills	College lecturer	5a
17 Mar.	Training on interactive whiteboards at college. Though the session was good the board they were using was different from the ones we have at school.	D. Smith	Trainer	5a

Assessor's comments

Miranda, your self-appraisal and appraisal provide very good evidence for this unit. Your diary of training events clearly shows how you have made effective use of developmental opportunities and support available to you.

Miranda, what you need to do next is to write up your personal goals for next year. Remember they need to be written in such a way that they can be seen as realistic, achievable, specific, measurable and time related.

Also have a look at the performance indicators for 2.4.1.

Signed: Terrie Cole

Terrie Cole
NVQ Assessor

Unit 2.4.1 Maintain working relationships with colleagues

Miranda looks at *some* of the performance indicators for Unit 2.4.1

Unit 2.4.1 Maintain working relationships with colleagues

Performance indicators	*Scope*
(1) Provide consistent and effective support for colleagues in line with the requirements and responsibilities of your role	(a) Those with whom you work on a frequent basis. (b) Those with whom you work on an occasional basis.
(2) Communicate openly and honestly with your colleagues	(a) Those with whom you work on a frequent basis. (b) Those with whom you work on an occasional basis.
(5) Accurately and fairly report any issues in your working relationships which cannot be resolved to someone who has the authority and capability to reach a resolution	(a) Poor communication (b) Conflicts

Miranda rereads her personal accounts in her portfolio and realises that she already has some evidence that can be used for this unit. The next week at college Miranda submits her evidence to her assessor.

Personal Account

Name: Miranda Appleton
Date: 22 March 2006
Year 3

Activity

As it was the week before Mother's day – the afternoon session was geared to making Mother's Day cards. Our regular class teacher was away on a training day and the student teacher was taking the class. The student teacher's college tutor was scheduled to come that day and to observe the student teacher's practice.

Before the pupils came in from afternoon break we assembled all of the material. The student teacher asked me to work with the two less able groups and to help them with writing a few lines of thank you to their mothers.

We had the paints out. We had bits of flowered material, ribbons and lots of glitter. I suggested to the student teacher that the pupils take it in turns to use the sink in the classroom to clean up after the task rather than go to the toilets at the other end of the hall.

The student teacher said no – the pupils could use the toilets at the end of the hall as this would be quicker than everyone taking their turn and that she wanted to finish this task as quickly as possible so she could move on to some more numeracy work. I tried to suggest to her that actually using the sink would be the better option but she told me to do what I was told and to work with the two less able groups.

I did what I was instructed to do – and when it came to cleaning up time I allowed the children to go to the toilets down the hall.

Well, it was a mess. Some pupils just love glitter and not only did we have glitter all over the classroom, it was now all over the corridor leading to the toilets and on the walls and all over the sinks in the toilet. Well Miss Smith came out of her class and yelled at the pupils for making such a mess. To make matters worse John Smith, in collecting the paint trays, tripped and dropped the paint trays all over the college tutor's lap.

Obviously things did not go well for the student teacher, what with her college tutor and all. The student teacher came up to me later and said that she was really disappointed in me and that she had expected me to be more helpful and that she would be having words with my teacher.

I was very upset by this and talked to the class teacher when she got back.

Signature: Miranda Appleton Date: 24 March 2006

Teacher's comments

I had words with the student teacher the next day. Usually the student teacher is very capable and very good at working with other staff members. I think her nerves at being assessed by the college tutor got the better of her. After calming down, the student teacher apologised to Miranda.

M. Higglesmith (Class Teacher) 24 March 2006

Assessor's comments

Well done – on your personal development plan. Remember to come back to this and update as necessary. For example when you have attended the first aid course – include relevant certificates in your portfolio.

As for the personal account – how unfortunate for you. However disagreements at school do happen.

On the bright side this personal account does meet many performance indicators for dealing effectively with colleagues. (Element 2.4.1, 1b, 2ab, 5ab)

Again, remember confidentiality.

Rereading your personal accounts to see if they can be cross-referenced to other units is always a good strategy. Well done!

Signed: Terrie Cole

Terrie Cole
NVQ Assessor

My personal development plan: Miranda Appleton

After rereading my self-appraisal and appraisal and reflecting on the comments made I set myself personal goals to improve my practice as a TA.

These goals are realistic, achievable, specific, measurable and time related.

Goals	*What I need to do to meet my goal*	*Measurable* *I will know that I have reached my goal when*	*Time-related* *I hope to achieve this goal by:*
To feel more confident when dealing with pupils who act up	Attend further INSET days on behaviour management Talk to senior TA at school or class teacher if I am having difficulties with a pupil.	I feel more confident in the class-room and will not have to always go to the teacher for assistance. I know what situations I need to go to her for help and which situations I can deal with by myself.	I am giving myself another year. By then I will feel more established within the school.
To attend required training on computers	Look at relevant courses on offer at college and sign up for suitable course.	I can deal with minor computer problems by myself.	Spring 2007
To gain a qualification in first aid	The school has enrolled me on a course starting the end of June.	I have gained a first aid qualification.	June 2006
To attend training on interactive whiteboards	To talk to ICT coordinator.	I feel confident on a whiteboard.	Spring 2007
To finish the NVQ 2 course	Continue putting together my portfolio.	I have finished and I have been awarded the certificate.	July hopefully!

Chapter 6

Unit 2.5.1 Support literacy activities in the classroom

The first part of Unit 2.5 considers activities to support literacy.

KNOWLEDGE BASE

2.5.1 Support literacy activities in the classroom

Policies and publications

You need to read your school's policy for literacy which should set out the overall vision for literacy, the objectives and reasons for teaching literacy, and outline the way literacy will be taught throughout the school. It will tie in with the National Curriculum, which sets out **Programmes of Study** of English for each of the Key Stages under the headings of speaking and listening (En1), reading (En2) and writing (En3). Attainment Targets are also given which set out what pupils must be able to do to reach each National Curriculum level. If you are working in a primary school, you need to show you are aware of the range of publications and policies relating to the **National Literacy Strategy (NLS)**.

How pupils develop reading, writing, speaking and listening skills and the factors that promote and hinder effective learning

Cognitive development

Just as there is physical development in children, so there is learning development – called *cognitive* development. An outline understanding of how children develop the skills they need to make progress in literacy will help in supporting them.

Speaking and listening

We learn how to speak through imitating those around us. This has significant implications for school life. Some children begin school already using a wide range of words and being able to express themselves very well. Others have a much more limited vocabulary and means of saying what they want to say.

Reading and writing

Reading and writing do not come naturally; they have to be learnt and for pupils to learn these skills, they need to be *taught* them. Neither reading nor writing is gained merely through imitation.

Reading involves a combination of four processes – the experience of the child resulting in knowledge of what the book is about (content); skills at decoding (**phonics**); understanding of the structure of the language used (grammar) and being able to read words on sight (word recognition).

Children learn from others. They make progress not only through their own natural development but also through interaction with others, particularly significant adults who teach them the skills and the knowledge they need to make that progress. Children need to be taught to read and write using apparatus that they can see and touch before they can progress onto more abstract ways of learning. This is called **multi-sensory** teaching and is a crucial part of most reading programmes.

The visual impact of the text is important. Children can be helped to make sense of texts by the use of pictures, suitable print size, the spacing of lines, the amount of words on a page, the complexity of sentences and the type of font used.

The literacy skills expected of the pupils with whom you work

Class teachers will have targets towards which each pupil in their class will be working. For the majority of pupils these targets will be in line with the National Curriculum Level Descriptors appropriate for their age range. Some pupils will be working ahead of the expected levels for their age group while others are going to be working at lower levels.

Those who are two or more terms behind are likely to have been identified as having special educational needs. In this case they will have Individual Educational Plans, which will indicate the targets towards which they are working.

You can find out about the literacy skills expected of the pupils with whom you work by looking at the class records, including IEPs, reading the National Curriculum Level Descriptors and through discussion with the class teacher or the school's Special Educational Needs Coordinator.

Special educational needs and their implications for literacy

Not all children find learning to read and write easy. Teachers will keep records relating to the special needs of pupils in their classes which should indicate both the nature of the need and the level of difficulty experienced in that area. These records will have been drawn up in consultation with the school's SENCO and will normally be in the form of IEPs.

The implications of pupils' special needs are many and varied. For instance, pupils with a specific learning difficulty, such as **dyslexia**, may well be functioning within the average or above average range for science and numeracy, but struggle with reading and spelling. Other pupils may have plenty of ideas to write about and can structure a story verbally using a range of vocabulary but find it extremely difficult to physically write the words as they have **dyspraxia** (more correctly termed

Development Coordination Disorder). Those pupils who have an all-round global developmental delay may be functioning at two years or more below the level of most of their peer group in all areas of the curriculum, while other pupils are academically above average but are held back by challenging behaviour or disturbed emotions. Still others will experience physical or sensory impairments which impact on their learning to a greater or lesser extent.

Discussion with your class teacher and the SENCO and reading the pupils' IEPs should give you a clear understanding of the impact that special educational needs has on the learning of the pupils you are being asked to work with.

Strategies used by the school for supporting literacy development

National Literacy Strategy

The majority of primary schools follow this strategy. Several publications relate to the NLS which you need to see – *the National Literacy Strategy Framework of Teaching Objectives, Progression in Phonics, The Spelling Bank, Early Literacy Support (ELS), Additional Literacy Support (ALS), Further Literacy Support (FLS), Grammar for Writing,* and *Revision Guidance for Y6 pupils.* All of these are published by the government and should be available via your class teacher or through the school's literacy coordinator.

Literacy Hour

A major part of the NLS is the daily Literacy Hour, which is divided into four main sections:

- *Shared text work*, when the teacher works with the whole class looking at texts and through this teaches reading and/or writing skills.
- *Shared word/sentence work*, when the teacher works with the whole class on phonics, spelling, grammar and/or punctuation.
- *Guided/independent work*, when the class is divided into groups and the teacher and teaching assistant each work with a group of children on reading or writing while the rest of the class work independently.
- *The plenary session*, when the whole class gathers together to discuss the lessons learnt.

Intervention programmes

For individual pupils and small groups there are numerous intervention programmes on the market. These include reading schemes, phonic schemes, spelling programmes, and activities to promote **phonological awareness**, social skills and speaking and listening skills.

Framework for Teaching English

This is the national strategy covering the teaching of English in Key Stage 3. As for the Primary Literacy Strategy, it divides the subject into word level, sentence level and text level work and recommends what should be taught in each year group. Although there is no equivalent of the literacy hour, there is a suggested lesson structure given in the Framework. TAs working in the secondary sector need to be familiar with this Framework if they are supporting students in English.

Interactive use of listening, speaking, reading and writing to promote literacy development in pupils

Students should leave school being able to communicate with a wide range of people in a variety of ways. No one aspect of literacy is more important than any other and this should be reflected in the teaching provided for children of whatever age. Your role as a teaching assistant is part of the process of developing these interactive skills.

You can encourage timid or reticent pupils to share their ideas. You can help impetuous or impatient pupils to wait and listen before they leap into action. You can help pupils generalise their knowledge by saying something like, 'You remember what we talked about yesterday? Well, this passage is about the same thing.' You have opportunities to help pupils recognise the connection between what they hear and say, what they read and what they write (see Figure 6.1).

How to use praise and assistance to maintain pupils' interest in and enthusiasm for understanding and using the full scope of literacy skills

Giving praise

Learning to read and write is a complex and difficult process and every opportunity needs to be given to praise and commend pupils' efforts as well as their progress.

Verbal praise

Verbal praise from someone the child respects is crucial. Many reading programmes state the need for '*pause-prompt-praise*' when listening to younger children read. If they get stuck on a word, pause for ten seconds to give them opportunity to work it out; prompt them perhaps with the initial sound or pointing out the context; then praise them for their effort.

Marking work

Written praise is also important – particularly as the children get older. Marking books may be the bane of teachers' lives, but it can be an effective tool in helping pupils learn. If you are asked to mark books, always begin by praising what is right – be specific and be accurate. For instance, you could write something like this: '*I like your idea of the green fairy coming out of the egg – but what happened then?*' (This could be written on a piece of work where there is a story opening, but the pupil has not continued with any other ideas.)

Figure 6.1 TAs can encourage reading in the pupils they support

Reward systems

Stickers and certificates are used in most primary schools to acknowledge good work and effort. It is important to recognise both the results of the work and the effort put into it. A child who is naturally gifted at writing may have produced an excellent piece of work, but actually may have not worked as hard as the child who has struggled to put two sentences together; the effort of the latter needs to be praised and rewarded as much, if not more, than the results of the former.

Praise reinforces progress. It makes us feel good about ourselves and makes us feel that what we are doing is worthwhile.

Giving assistance: striking the right balance

At one and the same time you want to help children learn, yet you also want to promote their independence. You are not there to do the work for the child, neither are you there simply as an observer to note down their mistakes. Somewhere in between is the 'happy medium'.

Techniques for giving assistance

A whole range of techniques are available to you as you seek to assist children develop their literacy skills. Some of these include asking questions, presenting choices, offering suggestions, reminding pupils of what they have previously learnt, or pointing them in the direction of aids to learning such as dictionaries.

Boosting confidence and self-esteem

Giving assistance, perhaps above all else, involves giving the child the confidence that they can tackle a task. 'Yes, you can do it,' is worth a lot. As with praise, this must be realistic. It is important to have a positive attitude yourself towards the pupils and their learning as this will rub off on them. If they feel that you believe in them, they are more likely to make progress and maintain their own enthusiasm.

Communicating with the teacher

You need to tell the class teacher if the tasks given to the pupils you are working with are too easy or too hard. Enthusiasm is curtailed both through boredom or being asked to do the impossible. Giving assistance to pupils therefore involves you communicating this sort of information to those who have the responsibility for teaching those pupils.

Checklist

- ✔ I am familiar with the strategies used to teach literacy in my school.
- ✔ I am aware of the special educational needs of the pupils I work with and am familiar with the resources available to support them.
- ✔ I understand the necessity of giving meaningful praise to pupils.
- ✔ I use a range of strategies to both support pupils and boost their confidence and independent skills.

MEETING PERFORMANCE INDICATORS

2.5.1 Support literary activities in the classroom

Setting the scene

Reading intervention programme with Year 5 pupils

Miranda is sitting at a table with six pupils within the class during the guided reading group work part of the literacy hour. The group is using a published special needs reading scheme. Each pupil is at least two terms behind the expected norm, some are more than a year behind and one is almost two years behind.

The lesson and TA support

Miranda: Let's look back at what we read last time. Can anyone tell me what the chapter was about?

[Members of the group give suitable answers.]

Miranda: Very good. Now we are going to read the next chapter together. First look at the pictures and tell me what you think is going to happen in this chapter.

[The group do so.]

Miranda: Now we are going to read this together, one page at a time beginning with Billy. We'll go round the group so that everybody gets a turn . . .

[As the group each take turns in reading the chapter out loud, Miranda uses *pause-prompt-praise* to teach reading skills. All but one of the pupils is reading fluently with this type of support. The pupil who is almost two years behind with his reading struggles with a quarter of the words.]

Miranda: Now we are going to answer questions on the chapter to make sure we all understand it. [She gives out worksheets.] Let's read the questions together then you can write your own answers.

The remainder of the lesson is spent with pupils working individually writing on the worksheets to answer the questions on the text. Although Miranda seeks to support all six pupils during the writing activity, she needs to spend much of her time with the pupil who struggles the most.

Writing personal accounts: covering performance indicators

Miranda did a lot to help the group, but she is just starting on her course and finds it difficult to write her personal account to show what she did in a way which links in with NVQ performance indicators, even though she writes the performance indicators in full next to her personal account.

Activity: Year 5 reading group in the literacy hour

Personal Account

Name: Miranda Appleton
Date: 4 October 2005
2.5.1 Support literacy activities in the classroom

Obtained up-to-date information from the class teacher on the learning objectives of the activity

Help pupils learn to read. I know this because it is what the whole programme is about.

Activity to be undertaken

The pupils will read aloud, discuss the story, answer questions on the book and discuss their answers.

Obtained up-to-date information from the class teacher on the type of support I am to give

I will lead the group – deciding who is to read and what they are to read. I will instruct them in the written work. I will help them with spellings and with putting their answers into sentences. I will chair the discussion making sure that everyone has a chance to say something.

Obtained up-to-date information from the teacher on the teacher's expectations of the pupils' current literacy skills

I have not discussed this group with the teacher for a while, but when it was set up the teacher told me that they all found reading difficult.

Offered the required types of support as and when needed by the pupil

I did what I planned to do. It is what I do twice a week with the group and it seems to work.

Given encouragement and feedback using vocabulary which the pupil is likely to understand

I encouraged all the pupils to have a go at reading. There is one pupil who struggles a lot with reading. He doesn't like doing it and he certainly does not like to read out loud. I sat next to him, showing by my body language that I thought he could do it. He was willing to read one page of the book out loud. I prompted him with words he did not know and he read most of them by himself.

When the pupils talked about the book or spoke out their answers I asked them questions to draw them out more. I praised them when they were on the right track, which was most of the time. If they were uncertain I did not tell them they were wrong but encouraged them to look at specific sentences or words.

Provided the teacher with relevant feedback on the progress of the activity and the pupil's response to it

I keep a written record of what we do in the group. The teacher looks at this if she wants to. If there is something seriously wrong then I will speak with her.

You have begun to reflect on the activity. Well done.

What went well

I think the group works well. They like being able to read at their level and in a small group where they don't have to speak up in front of a large class. They have more confidence in this group.

What I was not happy with

The greatest issue is needing to spend so much time with the pupil who is really struggling. In some ways he should not be in the group. He would be better off being taught one to one – but there is nobody to do it. Thinking about it though, I could support him more by choosing a page for him to read before the lesson and going over it with him so that he can read it aloud without my help. I'll try this next time.

You are using your experience in one lesson to shape what could happen in further lessons.

What I would do differently next time

I will lead the group in the same way, but I will prepare the struggling reader before like I said.

Teacher's comments

Miranda worked well with the group. I have every confidence in her ability to lead the group and to teach them well.

I certify that this is a true statement of what occurred.

Teacher's signature   Name (printed and role)
Mrs Disraeli   Emily Disraeli, Y5 Class Teacher

Assessor's comments

You clearly know what you are doing and what the group is capable of. You did a great deal during that half hour, but much of it you have not mentioned. It is almost like having to 'read between the lines' to find out all the things you actually did to give support. Though you have used the performance indicators as subheadings, you have not included enough detail to show that you met the performance indicators.

You need to think about the learning objective. Following a set programme can give a sense of security, both to you and to the group, but it is important to know exactly what is trying to be achieved in each lesson. Again, refer to the words used in the performance indicators for this.

Feedback to the teacher seems to be a bit hit and miss. How do you and the teacher know what progress the pupils are making? How do you know that they are making progress at the right pace? Some mention of this as an area to develop would be useful. Include details of your ongoing records as evidence.

Signed: Terrie Cole

Terrie Cole
NVQ Assessor

Let's look at how Miranda could have written this: here is her second attempt.

Activity: Year 5 reading group in the literacy hour

Personal Account

Name: Miranda Appleton
Date: 4 October 2005
2.5.1 Support literacy activities in the classroom

You are much more specific about the activity.

Context of the lesson/activity

Working with group of six pupils within the classroom. Using *Starstruck* reading scheme – part of programme to develop their reading. This is done twice a week for half an hour as part of the Literacy Hour.

Obtained up-to-date information from the class teacher on the learning objectives of the activity

The class teacher had shown me her plans for the week and at the beginning of the session had discussed with me what she wanted the pupils to achieve in their reading during the session. Overall this was to develop their sight vocabulary, phonic skills and comprehension skills so they can read with confidence, fluency and understanding.

Obtained up-to-date information from the class teacher on the type of support I am to give

During the half-hour lesson the pupils will read aloud, discuss the story, answer questions on the book and discuss their answers. They will seek information from the text and will share their ideas. Some of the questions are closed to show that they can gain specific information, others are open questions showing that they can understand the text and make judgements from it. For instance, I will ask something like, 'What happened when Jimmy lost his football?' (closed question) and 'How do you think Jane felt when Lucy did not come home that evening?' (open question).

I will lead the group – deciding who is to read and what they are to read. I will instruct them in the written work. I will give them examples of how they can answer the questions. I will help them with spellings and with putting their answers into sentences. I will chair the discussion making sure that every one has a chance to say something.

Obtained up-to-date information from the teacher on the teacher's expectations of the pupils' current literacy skills

I have not discussed this group with the teacher for a while, but when it was set up the teacher told me that they all found reading difficult. It may be useful to give each pupil a reading assessment so we know what their current reading age is. I will suggest this to the teacher.

Good to see you using actual terms from the performance indicators: 'shy and reticent pupils' and 'supportive audience'.

Offered the required types of support as and when needed by the pupil

I prompted reticent and shy pupils to read aloud. I made sure each pupil took part in any discussion. I explained words used in the book that some found hard to understand – I did this by using questions and examples rather than just telling them what it meant. Thinking about this we could look at dictionary skills in another lesson so they can find out the meanings of words for themselves. I will add this to the planning. This will help pupils to use resources relevant to the learning activity. Overall I provided a supportive audience both to the reading and to the discussion.

You are very specific about the kind of encouragement you gave. Well done. Perhaps you could have included why you used these strategies.

Given encouragement and feedback using vocabulary which the pupil is likely to understand

I encouraged all the pupils to have a go at reading. There is one pupil who struggles a lot with reading. He doesn't like doing it and he certainly does not like to read out loud. I sat next to him, showing by my body language that I thought he could do it. I had talked with him before the lesson, as I do most weeks, and he was willing to read one page of the book out loud. I prompted him with words he did not know and he read most of them by himself.

When the pupils talked about the book or gave their answers I asked them questions to draw them out more, such as 'Why do you think that?' or 'What tells you that your answer is correct?' I praised them when they were on the right track, which was most of the time. If they were uncertain I did not tell them they were wrong but encouraged them to look at specific sentences or words. Sometimes I told them what words meant.

Provided the teacher with relevant feedback on the progress of the activity and the pupils' response to it

I keep a written record of what we do in the group (see pro forma). The teacher looks at this if she wants to. If there is something seriously wrong then I will speak with her. This needs to be tightened up. I need to know that the pupils are making the progress expected of them. We have read three books now, but I could not really say that they can read more words and that they understand more than they did three weeks ago.

What went well

I think the group works well. They like being able to read at their level and in a small group where they don't have to speak up in front of a large class. They have more confidence in this size of group.

What I was not happy with

The greatest issue is needing to spend so much time with the pupil who is really struggling. In some ways he should not be in the group. He would be better off being taught one to one – but there is nobody to do it. Thinking about it though, I could support him more by choosing a page for him to read before the lesson and going over it with him before the group so that he can read it aloud without my help. I'll try this next time.

What I would do differently next time

I will lead the group in the same way, but I will prepare the struggling reader before like I said. I will also introduce dictionary skills to boost the children's ability to be independent learners rather than relying on me for support. I will also need to make sure we work at an appropriate pace and are not just coasting along. I need to have specific objectives for each lesson.

Anywhere Primary School

Feedback Form to Teachers

Name of Teaching Assistant:
Miranda Appleton

Date: 4.10.05

Lesson: Y5 literacy

Activity: Small group work in class – reading and comprehension

Names of pupils:
Billy; Jean; Serendha;
Nicholas; John; Eric

Resources used:
Starstruck scheme level 4
reading books and comprehension pupil worksheets

Learning objective(s):

Develop sight vocabulary
Develop phonic skills
Develop comprehension skills

Overall levels of achievement (1–5 where 1 is not at all and 5 is totally achieved):

All group except Nicholas:
Sight vocabulary: 3
Phonic skills: 3
Comprehension: 3
Nicholas: 2 or even 1 for each

Comments about any individual pupil or particular aspects of the activity:
The group work well together and enjoy the activity. They are growing in confidence in reading. It is hard to say exactly how much progress they make each lesson. Nicholas is really struggling.

Signature of TA: Miranda Appleton **Date:** 4.10.05

Teacher's comments

Miranda worked well with the group. I have every confidence in her ability to lead the group and to teach them well. Before the session I sat down with Miranda and we looked at the pupils' previous records of achievement. This helped Miranda to focus on their current literacy skills and to get a sense of what they were working towards. We discussed in detail the learning objective of the lesson. During the session I observed Miranda modelling correct use of vocabulary (e.g. when commenting on the passage, one pupil said, 'He done well there, didn't he miss?' and Miranda replied, 'Yes, he did well didn't he?'). I heard her explaining words and phrases I had used in the initial input to the class with her group (e.g. 'When Mrs Disraeli said, "I want us all to think about inferential questions in our reading" she means she wants us to think about why things happen in the story we read and how it makes people feel.'). She is right when she says that we need to 'tighten up' on how we record the progress of this group.

Teacher's signature	Name (printed and role)
Mrs Disraeli	Emily Disraeli, Y5 Class Teacher

Assessor's comments

This is much better. This personal account clearly shows you have met the performance indicators. Your teacher's feedback is extremely valuable, especially as her comments are targeted at the specific performance indicators. It is always a good idea to discuss with your teacher what you are hoping to achieve. Well done on including your feedback forms. Again, this is good supporting evidence.

Signed: Terrie Cole

Terrie Cole
NVQ Assessor

Chapter 7

Unit 2.5.2 Support numeracy activities in the classroom

The second part of Unit 2.5 considers activities to support numeracy.

KNOWLEDGE BASE

2.5.2 Support numeracy activities in the classroom

The school policy for mathematics and how this relates to national and local policies and frameworks for mathematics

School mathematics policies will differ in their details, but all primary school policies should make reference to the **National Numeracy Strategy** (NNS), stating how it will be implemented throughout the school. You need to be familiar with both your school's policy and with the basics of the NNS. For secondary schools, the government has introduced the *Framework for Teaching Mathematics in Years 7, 8 and 9* as part of the Key Stage 3 National Strategy. The aim of the framework is to help secondary schools build on and follow on from the NNS and to improve transition from primary to secondary schools. If you are supporting mathematics in Key Stage 3, you will need to be familiar with this framework.

National Numeracy Strategy

The NNS is a government initiative aiming to enhance the learning of mathematics within primary schools. Between 45 minutes and one hour each day is to be given over to teaching maths in a structured way, combining whole class teaching, individual or group work and whole class discussion to review and reinforce the learning that has taken place. A number of mathematical objectives which should be achieved by the majority of pupils in any particular year group are identified, but teachers are encouraged to work towards objectives from other year groups in order to meet the needs of their pupils.

How pupils develop mathematical skills and the factors that promote and hinder effective learning

Pupils move through stages of needing 'real' apparatus, such as small toys, beads, plastic or wooden blocks; then equipment such as number lines and number fans, before being able to think more abstractly. Pupils will move through these stages at different rates, and the NNS makes provision for this.

Confidence is important in learning any subject, but perhaps especially so for maths. Many children and adults too are simply scared of maths and freeze at the thought of doing it. If you are to support pupils struggling with maths, this lack of confidence must be overcome (see Figure 7.1).

Confidence is promoted by success. We feel good about what we are good at. To boost confidence in maths, pupils must be given tasks which they can do rather than activities which are always too difficult for them.

Why is maths particularly difficult for some pupils?

Maths can present significant difficulties to children:

- The range of vocabulary and the number of alternative methods available to solve any one problem may cause confusion, for example 'add', 'total' and 'sum' are three different words, but all refer to essentially the same mathematical operation.
- Some pupils will find it hard to remember all the pieces of information and steps required to solve a problem or complete a calculation.
- The speed or pace of the lesson may be too fast for some children and they get left behind.

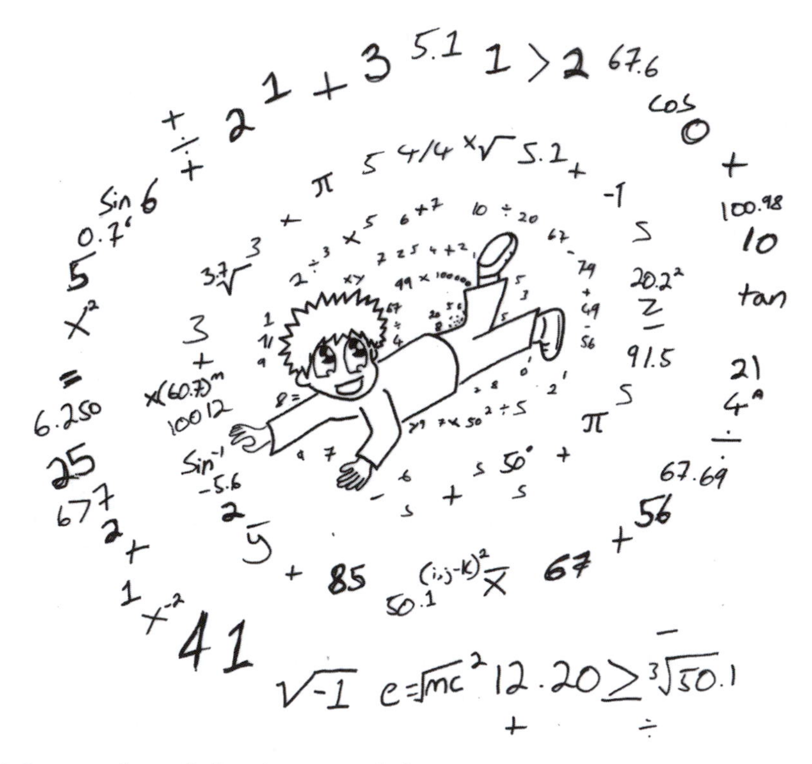

Figure 7.1 Some pupils can find maths an overwhelming experience

- Pupils may have to move onto a new topic before they have fully understood the current one.
- There may not be sufficient use of concrete, 'hands-on' materials to enable children to fully understand the concepts being taught.
- Some pupils are able to do the maths, but struggle because they cannot read the questions or write down their answers.
- Maths can provoke panic, causing the brain to 'shut down' or the pupil to react aggressively.

The mathematical knowledge and skills expected of the pupils with whom you work

Continuous monitoring, observation and assessment will enable teachers and TAs to establish the exact understanding of the pupils in their classes. Formal tests, including national testing, gives some indication of the level of understanding. However asking questions of the pupils individually or in small groups about what they are doing in maths will yield a depth of information possibly not gained through testing. Asking a pupil how they found out that 28 multiplied by 3 gave an answer of 84 will tell a lot about their thinking processes and underlying mathematical understanding. For instance, they may say that to get 28 multiplied by 3 you need to add 28 and 28 and 28. This shows they understand something about multiplication being continuous addition. However, if this is the only method they know, it is very laborious and they will take a long time completing more complex multiplication calculations.

There needs to be a thorough understanding of the level of mathematical understanding and knowledge held by pupils in a class before valid judgements can be made regarding their expected level of functioning.

Part of your role as a TA could be to ask these sorts of questions, the most effective of which may well be, 'Tell me how you came to that answer.' You are also there to record pupils' responses and pass these on to the teacher.

The nature of any special educational needs of pupils with whom you work and the implications of these for helping them to develop mathematical knowledge, understanding and skills

The types of special need encountered by the pupils with whom you work will be outlined to you by the class teacher and/or the SENCO. You will need to read their IEPs to gain more information. However, some general principles apply to supporting pupils in mathematics who experience a range of barriers to their learning.

What you can do

- Help pupils understand what is being said by repeating it in simplified language.
- Help the pupil frame or formulate their own answers by asking questions such as, 'How could you explain that?' or 'Why do you think you got that answer?'
- Remind them of what they have learnt previously.
- Use visual stimuli and concrete apparatus such as games, number lines, multilink.
- Keep a pupil who is easily distracted focused on the lesson.

- Ensure that all pupils understand what is being asked of them and can read any materials that have been handed out.
- Go over the teaching points already made in the lesson, taking time to give more explanation if needed.
- Provide adapted resources, including work in large print.
- Work with pupils using ICT.
- Prepare pupils to participate in the plenary by going over their answers with them, asking them for their ideas and suggestions and encouraging them to speak up in the class discussion.
- Agree strategies with the teacher for including those children who find numeracy difficult.

You are likely to use structured, cumulative (i.e. one fact or skill building upon another) and multi-sensory methods when seeking to develop numerical understanding.

Not too much at once

It is better to focus on a limited amount which can be understood, than try to teach everything and end up with the pupil confused. For instance, you may be supporting a pupil who finds it hard to process information quickly. During a mental maths session, therefore, where the class are required to answer ten or twenty questions within a certain time frame, you could encourage them to try and answer every other question. This will give them the opportunity to get at least half right, rather than seek to attempt all of them and, most probably, get most or all of them wrong.

'Can you explain how you did this?'

Asking pupils to talk about how they approached certain problems or arrived at particular conclusions is an important element of TA support. It may be that, by listening to what they say, you can see why pupils are making errors and can teach to that gap or misunderstanding. If, say, a pupil tells you that they worked out that 16 plus 23 made 48, it may be that they are confusing the digits in the tens and units columns and you can teach specifically to this. This is more likely to be the case if they are adding in lines rather than columns (16 + 23 = ___). They may look at the first digit in the calculation (1) and add that to the last digit (3), then they may add the middle two digits (6 and 2) thus deciding the answer to the question is 48 (1+3 and 6+2).

Ensure the basics are in place

As pupils get older and begin to experience difficulties in maths, it is tempting to try and tackle the immediate presenting problem. This, in itself, may well be insufficient. You need to check that the pupil has a grasp of fundamental language such as 'bigger than, smaller than, first, second, after'. You also need to make sure that they appreciate that sometimes different terminology means essentially the same thing; that, for example, 'subtraction,' 'difference' and 'minus' relate to essentially the same mathematical calculation.

Use concrete apparatus

Whatever a pupil's abilities in maths, using concrete materials can effectively introduce or consolidate concepts. Number lines and number squares, while being useful, rely solely on visual skills. More tactile equipment such as plastic or wooden cubes and rods are readily available in primary schools and in special needs departments of secondary schools.

Constant review

'Use it or lose it' certainly applies to maths, and is especially significant as some mathematical concepts are visited only infrequently in the NNS. You can support pupils by ensuring concepts and facts they have been taught are regularly and frequently reviewed.

Little and often

The key is 'little and often'. Ten minutes each day with individuals or a small group using memory cards, physical apparatus or whatever to reinforce, consolidate and generalise mathematical concepts and facts is far better than an hour each week of such activities. This may be hard to organise, but it is well worth it.

The strategies used at your school for supporting the development of mathematical knowledge, understanding and skills

Your school's maths policy will outline the strategies used in the school to support the development of mathematical knowledge, understanding and skills. This may or may not include the use of a published maths scheme; some schools choose to dip in and out of a range of schemes rather than just follow one. The policy is likely to refer to **differentiation** within lessons and possibly the subsequent setting into ability groups.

All schools are likely to deploy TAs as part of their strategy for supporting numeracy development. Some will focus purely on supporting pupils who are struggling in this area, others may deploy additional adults to stretch the more able pupils while still others ask TAs to support the whole range of abilities.

There is also likely to be mention of the way maths resources are to be used throughout the school, including the use of ICT. Reference may be made to published maths schemes or to software programs available either on the school intranet or on websites which are suitable at different levels for the various aspects of mathematics such as learning to tell the time; comparing fractions, decimals and percentages; or establishing basic concepts of geometry.

The sorts of resources used to help pupils to develop knowledge, understanding and skills in mathematics

All pupils begin by using concrete, practical apparatus and many will need to continue with this for a number of years, some throughout their primary school years and into secondary school. A vast number of resources are available on the market – you need to find out what resources are available in your school, how they are to be used and where they are stored.

Popular resources include coloured plastic cubes (multilink), Dienes blocks, Cuisenaire rods and Numicon. All seek to teach the concept of number rather than simply support calculations and the manipulation of number.

To develop an understanding of space, shape and measure pupils will need to have access to a range of physical apparatus such as two-dimensional and three-dimensional shapes, protractors, rulers, pairs of compasses and set squares.

How to use praise and assistance to maintain the pupils' interest in and enthusiasm for understanding and using mathematics

Pupils respond to praise – but praise must be genuine and specific. Praise for numeracy is possibly more important than for other subjects as confidence levels can be low and difficult to achieve. Praise is a powerful way of boosting self-esteem. Saying 'well done' to pupils being supported goes a long way, but it must be specific, e.g. 'Well done, you have remembered your multiplication table of seven and are using this in your calculations.'

Enthusiasm is contagious – you can say what you like to the children, but if you yourself dread maths, or at least feel ambivalent towards it, that is what they will pick up on. Your own attitude and approach to numeracy is therefore vital when you seek to support pupils.

Checklist

- ✔ I am familiar with the strategies used in my school to teach mathematics.
- ✔ I am aware of some of the difficulties experienced by pupils when they seek to make progress in mathematics.
- ✔ I appreciate the value of asking questions when supporting pupils in mathematics.
- ✔ I am aware of the special educational needs experienced by pupils I am working with and of the resources available to support them.
- ✔ I am aware of the importance of giving meaningful praise in boosting confidence in mathematics.

MEETING PERFORMANCE INDICATORS

2.5.2 Support numeracy activities in the classroom

Setting the scene

Nicola is working in a Year 7 lower numeracy set where the students are continuing to struggle with concepts of multiplication. It is the first lesson in a new maths topic. The learning objective is to use the grid method to multiply tens and units by units using facts from the 3, 7 and 8 multiplication tables. The first part of the lesson is input from the teacher, Miss Salisbury, who uses an **interactive whiteboard** to explain how to use the grid method to solve multiplication questions. This is followed by a whole class activity with pupils working independently practising the procedure being taught. The teacher puts ten questions on the board which the pupils are to try and calculate. There is a plenary towards the end of the lesson when pupils share their answers and the final activity is a card game played in groups to reinforce multiplication facts.

Writing personal accounts: covering performance indicators

When writing up what she has done, Nicola makes reference to the following performance indicators. They do not cover all that is required to meet the standard for this unit and she will need to present a number of pieces of evidence to achieve this.

Unit 2.5.2 Support numeracy activities in the classroom

Performance indicators	*Scope*
(1) Obtain up-to-date information from the teacher on: • the *learning objectives* of the activity • the *types of support* you are to give • the teacher's expectations of the *pupils'* current numeracy skills.	*Scope of learning objectives* (a) To understand and apply mental calculation strategies and written methods of calculation (b) To recall number facts (c) To use efficient calculations to solve problems (d) To use appropriate strategies for checking the results of calculations (e) To be able to explain methods and reasoning using correct mathematical language
(2) Offer the required *types of support* as and when needed by the *pupil*.	*Scope of type of support* (a) Prompting shy or reticent pupils (b) Practising number work (c) Helping pupils to use equipment and resources relevant to the learning activity (d) Reflecting and questioning choices made by the pupil (e) Translating or explaining words and phrases used by the teacher (f) Reminding pupils of teaching points made by the teacher

Performance indicators	*Scope*
	(g) Modelling correct use of mathematical language and vocabulary
	(h) Ensuring that pupils understand and follow the teacher's instructions
	(i) Organising and taking part in mathematical games
(3) Give encouragement and feedback using appropriate mathematical language and vocabulary which the *pupil* is likely to understand.	*Scope of pupils* (a) Working as part of a class group
(4) Provide the teacher with relevant feedback on the progress of the *activity* and the *pupils'* response to it.	*Scope of activities* (a) Counting, matching and sequencing activities

Personal Account

Name: Nicola Wilson
Date: 9 March 2006
2.5.2 Help pupils with activities which develop numeracy

This session deals with understanding and applying mental calculations and written methods of calculation; recalling number facts; and being able to explain methods and reasoning using correct mathematical language

Obtain up-to-date information from the teacher on the learning objectives of the activity

As I had seen Miss Salisbury's planning beforehand, I knew what the learning objective was. We had talked about it before the lesson so I knew what she was expecting from the class.

Obtain up-to-date information from the teacher on the types of support I gave

Miss Salisbury and I had discussed the type of support I was to give so that when it came to the actual lesson I did not need to be told what to do. It was agreed that I would make sure that all pupils had understood and were following the teacher's instructions and that they were using appropriate mathematical language and vocabulary.

Obtain up-to-date information on the teacher's expectations of the pupils' current numeracy skills

The previous week the class had been given a diagnostic numeracy test which Miss Salisbury had marked. She told me that this assessment showed that, while most pupils knew the multiplication tables 3, 7 and 8, they were uncertain about applying this knowledge when multiplying tens and units by units –hence this series of lessons.

Teacher's comments

I certify that this is a true statement of what occurred.

Teacher's signature	Name (printed and role)
N Salisbury	Miss N. Salisbury, Mathematics Teacher

What happened in the lesson itself could have been written up as a personal account. However, in this case, Nicola's assessor came to her school and sat in on the maths lesson making notes. Nicola said beforehand that she was anxious about having someone in the class observing her; but afterwards she commented that it wasn't that bad after all. In fact there were times when she forgot the assessor was there and when she saw all the performance indicators covered, she was thrilled. She even managed to provide evidence for her knowledge base by answering some questions from her assessor afterwards.

Observation Notes

Candidate: Nicola Wilson
Date: 9.3.06
School: Wherever Secondary School

2.5.2 Help pupils with activities which develop numeracy	**Performance indicators observed**
During teacher input	
The class were sitting in their assigned places and Nicola moved to sit near specific pupils for a short period of time. Some of these pupils had special needs; others were learning English as an additional language (EAL). She ensured they were correctly setting out the tens and units on their personal whiteboards as directed by Miss Salisbury. (A copy of the multiplication grid is attached.) She looked at what they were writing and listened to their answers to make sure that they were following the procedures and using multiplication facts correctly.	*Offered the required types of support as and when needed by the pupil* *Ensured that pupils understood and followed the teacher's instructions*
When she saw some struggling she quietly asked them questions or made suggestions about the task. She did not tell them what they should do. She repeated or simplified the teacher's instructions, using rephrasing techniques such as, '7 multiplied by 2, that's the same as 7 add 7, isn't it?'	*Translated or explained words and phrases used by the teacher*

Several of the pupils were getting correct answers but were reluctant to put their hands up in response to the teacher's questions. Nicola encouraged them to respond by saying things like, 'Go on, have a go' or 'I know you can do it.' She also encouraged them by her body language, such as giving them the 'thumbs up' sign.

Prompted shy or reticent pupils

During independent work

Nicola made sure that all pupils could see the board with the learning objective and follow-up questions on. She wrote the learning objective on a personal whiteboard for one pupil to copy who could not easily see the board from where she was sitting. She then moved to another pupil and reinforced the procedure that Miss Salisbury had taught.

Reminded pupils of teaching points made by the teacher

Then she went to a third pupil. Later Nicola told me that this pupil usually took a long time with her writing and she wrote the learning objective for her so the pupil could get on with the numeracy task immediately.

As she went round the class, several pupils asked Nicola questions such as, 'Is this right, miss?' or 'What do I do now?' In response to these she asked questions of her own, such as, 'What do you think?' or 'How can you check it?' She clearly wanted to build their independence and boost their ability to reflect on their own work.

Reflected and questioned choices made by the pupil

A good number of pupils were able to follow the procedure and use the grid method correctly, but they struggled because they did not know the relevant multiplication facts securely enough to give immediate recall. Nicola helped them by getting them to write down the appropriate multiplication tables so that they could use these in their calculations and practise them later.

Practised number work

When they were finding answers to calculations involving multiplying by 10, many pupils told Nicola, 'You add a nought.' She reminded them that they need to use correct mathematical language and that, 'Adding a nought does not change a number – three add nought is three'. She said they should rather be using vocabulary such as 'When multiplying by 10 the numbers move to the next higher column.'

Modelled correct use of mathematical language and vocabulary

During the plenary and reinforcement activity

Nicola encouraged shy and reticent pupils to give their answers to the rest of the class and talk about the work they had done. She realised that most had begun to understand the procedure and were accurately using some multiplication facts. She therefore said to several by name, 'Go on, so and so, I've seen you've done it well – why don't you share it with the rest of us?'

Prompted shy or reticent pupils

Towards the end of the plenary Nicola distributed cards with multiplication facts to each table so that the pupils could be ready to play multiplication pairs when they returned to their places. She told me afterwards that this is what Miss Salisbury had asked her to do. Nicola sat down at one table and joined in their game. Afterwards she told me she chose to sit next to a pupil, who can get quite excited and try to dominate the game, as she wanted to make sure he participated appropriately. At the end of the lesson she collected all the cards and returned them to their boxes.

Throughout the lesson I noted that Nicola was careful to use appropriate mathematical language when she spoke with the pupils and with Miss Salisbury; for example, using the term 'multiplication' rather than 'times'. She made a point of saying 'well done' to all the pupils she supported, specifying what it was they had done well, e.g. 'Well done, you have remembered your multiplication tables of seven and are using this in your calculations.'

Gave encouragement and feedback using appropriate mathematical language and vocabulary which the pupil is likely to understand

At the end of the plenary, along with Miss Salisbury, she praised all the class for their hard work and enthusiasm. Nicola specifically spoke with the pupils who were still struggling to understand the concepts being taught, praising them for their effort. Nicola said that lots of people find it hard to learn about multiplication, but that there were lots of ways to help them remember what to do which they would be looking at over the next few days.

Nicola's feedback to the class teacher

After the lesson I listened to Nicola feedback to the teacher. She told Miss Salisbury that she thought most pupils had understood what they should be doing, but named five or six who were still struggling. She suggested that, in the next lesson, these pupils might be given grid templates upon which they could work directly rather than be asked to draw their own grids in their books as they had done today. She felt this might give them more structure.

Provided the teacher with relevant feedback on the progress of the activity and the pupil's response to it

She also noted that, despite what was indicated by the previous week's assessment, many pupils were not fully secure in their multiplication tables and had to work out each calculation from scratch. One or two pupils were even confused about what the multiplication sign (×) meant – they initially thought it meant addition. There was, she thought, therefore a need to revisit these basics. She commented that, by and large, she thought the pupils had enjoyed the activity, even those who had struggled, because they could all see that they had learnt something. As it was only the first lesson in a series, she thought it went well and could easily be built upon.

Assessor's comments

A very effective session. I talked to Miss Salisbury afterwards and she stated that she was extremely appreciative of the help and support you offered.

Some questions which I would like to follow up with you:

- Do you have any SEN pupils with whom you work?
- If so, what allowances or support do you give to help them develop mathematical knowledge, understanding and skills?

Signed: Terrie Cole

Terrie Cole
NVQ Assessor

Chapter 8

Unit 3.1 Contribute to the management of pupil behaviour

In this unit there are two elements:

3.1.1 Promote school policies with regard to pupil behaviour
3.1.2 Support the implementation of strategies to manage pupil behaviour

KNOWLEDGE BASE

3.1.1 Promote school policies with regard to pupil behaviour

School policies which impact on behaviour management

Every school will have policies. School policies are not written in isolation but relate to local authority and national or government guidelines. The government is constantly rewriting old laws, drafting new laws, issuing guidance and disseminating, that is, giving examples of good practice. Some documents that are of interest to TAs are:

- The Children Act 2004
- *Every Child Matters* 2004
- Disability Discrimination Act 2005

See Chapters 12 and 13 for brief summaries of these documents and useful references.

In terms of behaviour management the school will have a policy on behaviour, bullying, child protection and equal opportunities. As a TA it is your role to get a copy of these policies and read them as they provide a wealth of information.

Roles and responsibilities of yourself and others within the school setting for managing pupils' behaviour

Schools aim to provide a safe, ordered and enriched environment where children can learn and reach their potential. In order for learning to take place behaviour needs to be managed. All school staff have a role to play in encouraging good behaviour and dealing effectively with disruptive behaviour. As a TA you will need to know what *you can do* to manage behaviour (see Figure 8.1). Specifically, you will need to know what strategies or techniques you can use. In addition you will need to know when to consult

Figure 8.1 Pupils' behaviour can sometimes present challenges

the teacher and what strategies the teacher alone can use. In order to know what your role is in managing behaviour you will need to discuss this with the other staff. To help you do this fill in a chart like the one that follows. (A template of this form can be found in the Appendix.) To help get you started let's look at how Miranda has started to fill in her chart (see pages 118–19).

Of course how you fill in this chart depends very much on your role. Your assessor will probably ask you questions in regard to what you can do as a TA and when you need to transfer responsibility to the teacher.

Procedures for managing pupils' negative behaviour

Encourage pupils to remember the rules

Remind pupils of the rules and expectations of behaviour before they begin an activity. If you notice a pupil misbehaving remind them of the rule or better still ask them to think about what they are doing. For example, ask the pupil: 'What are you doing? What should you be doing?'

Encourage pupils to think about how their behaviour affects other pupils

For example: 'I know that you wanted to use the ruler, but how do you think Tommy felt when you snatched the ruler from him?'

Encourage pupils to think about choices and consequences

For example if you are faced with a secondary pupil who is becoming rude to other pupils – you will need to remind the pupil of the expected behaviour in the class and the consequences, that is, a detention or being put on report for not behaving appropriately. Once you have informed the pupil about what happens if they do not do what they are told, then you tell them that it is their choice. This approach also encourages pupils to think about their behaviour.

If a reprimand is necessary – think about how you are going to give the reprimand

Sometimes it is helpful to ask the pupil to step outside or to come to the back of the classroom for a quiet chat. Important discussions are often best said in private. Giving a pupil a reprimand, or a telling off, in front of other class mates can sometimes backfire, as the pupil may feel under pressure to play to the audience.

In giving a reprimand it is important to consider the language you are using. You need to separate the behaviour from the person. Telling a pupil that they are 'naughty', 'a waste of space', 'that they will never amount to much' is not helpful; in fact it is counterproductive, in that, the pupil can come to believe this of themselves and start acting accordingly. So if as a TA you observe a child snatching a ruler – rather than saying 'You are naughty!' – you could say 'We have a rule for sharing in this classroom and I expect you to follow that rule – thank you'.

Another approach to managing negative behaviour is by taking steps to avoid the negative behaviour in the first place. As you spend time in a class you will begin to really know the pupils you are working with. You will learn which pupils work well together and likewise which pupils should not be placed together.

Promoting positive behaviour and dealing with negative behaviour requires teamwork! As a TA you have your role to play, but part of your role is to know when to ask for help and what incidents need to be brought to the attention of the teacher or head teacher.

The importance of rewarding positive behaviour and how to do this

Disruptive behaviour needs to be dealt with. However, the most effective way of dealing with disruptive or inappropriate behaviour is by encouraging and rewarding positive behaviour.

How to give praise

- Praise can be verbal. Praise can involve giving out a sticker or a house-point. Praise can involve informing the teacher of pupil achievements. This allows the teacher the opportunity to praise the pupil. Praise can involve writing glowing comments in their homework or reading diaries. To be effective, praise needs to be genuine. Praise also needs to be specific; that is, you need to tell the pupil what exactly it was that was good.
- Make sure the task set is achievable as it is easy to give praise to a child who achieves. If however you feel that the work set is too much for the pupil then you will need to discuss this with the teacher. Sometimes as a TA you might be able to adapt or modify the task so the pupil can achieve the work. This might mean going over points made by the teacher, using aides such as number lines, multilink or

Contribute to the management of pupil behaviour

Routine	*School and class rules*	*Role and responsibility of yourselves and others*			
	Pupils are expected to	*I (the TA) will intervene when*	*I (the TA) can use these strategies*	*I (the TA) will inform the teacher*	*The teacher will*
In the playground	• Play safely • Play kindly with other pupils • Stay in designated areas	• A child is in out of bounds area • Not playing safely on equipment or leaving equipment lying around so that it is a danger to others • If a child is alone	• Remind them of the rules for play • Remind them of the consequences of not behaving • Praise good behaviour • If a child is alone encourage them to play with others	• If a child refuses to behave after I have reminded them and told them of the consequences • Report any incidents of fighting, bullying or accidents	• The teacher has the authority to have pupils miss break and put their name in the red book
Standing outside in the corridor waiting to come into class	• Stand in separate lines • Class helpers to go to front of line • Whatever line is the quietest gets to come in first	• The pupils are making too much noise or pushing in their line	• Remind them of the rules, be quiet, no pushing • Praise good behaviour	• If a pupil refuses to get into line • If fighting occurs • If a pupil refuses to behave when asked	
Beginning of the day	• Enter quietly • Hang coats up • Put book bags in right box • Put lunch box on shelf in corridor • Put water bottle in tray • Sit quietly on carpet	• Remind pupils to hang their coats up • Remind pupils not to step on others' coats	• Praise for good behaviour	• Report to teacher if any pupil was upset	

Where to sit					
When wishing to participate in class					
When requesting help					
Going into assembly					
Walking in corridors					
Using ICT equipment					

dictionaries, or working through the questions with the pupil. If a pupil feels that they cannot do the work then the temptation for the pupil is to act up so that they do not have to do the work.

- Praising effort is important (see Figure 8.2). Praising effort increases the motivation to continue working at difficult problems. It is not whether the pupil gets the question right or wrong but the effort that they put into their work which is important. Getting stuck on a problem, realising that you don't understand is an uncomfortable but necessary part of learning. To learn new information you first need to realise that there are things that you don't know.

The importance of giving praise

- Praise gives pupil a feel good factor. Praise raises self-esteem.
- Praise is a powerful reward. Praise encourages the pupil to repeat that behaviour again.
- Praise motivates a pupil to work.
- When you praise a pupil, other pupils might imitate the behaviour so they too can be praised.

The scope and implications of factors that impact on the behaviour of all pupils

Many factors impact on the behaviour of all pupils, as shown in the diagram oppposite.

Figure 8.2 'Gurdit, I see you have been good today'

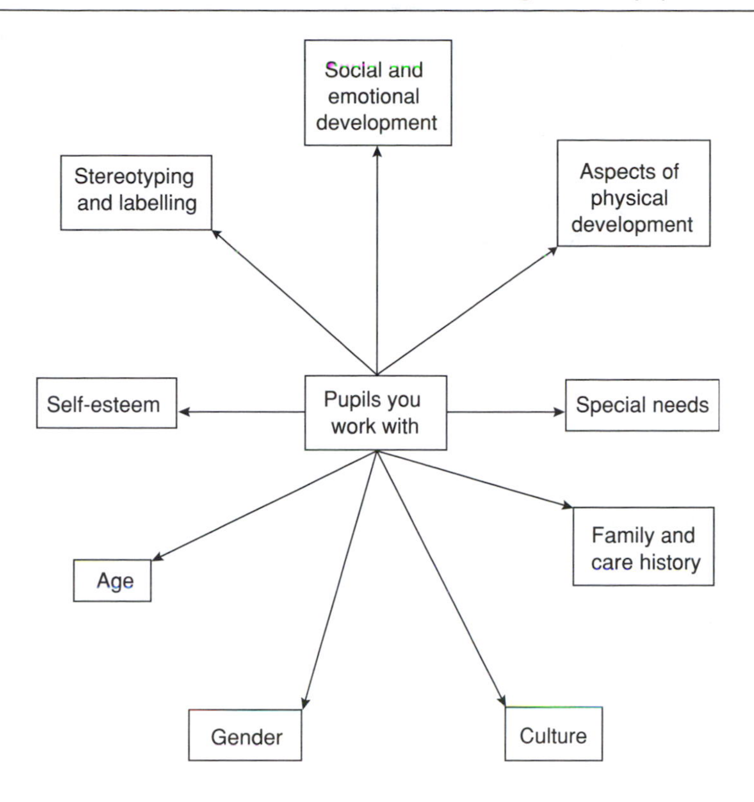

Social and emotional development

As children grow they learn how to relate to others around them and how to recognise and deal with their own emotions and those of others. When psychologists talk about social and emotional development they are talking about age-related changes in empathy (showing concern for others), sharing, turn-taking and friendship skills.

Aspects of physical development

Professionals often refer to what is known as milestones in physical development. For example, the average child will start to walk from anywhere between 10 months and 18 months. A knowledge of physical milestones is important as children who are delayed in reaching their physical milestones might need additional help.

Special needs

Special needs has been defined as occurring when a child has significantly greater difficulty in learning than the majority of other children of his/her age; or has a disability which prevents or hinders the child from making use of the educational facilities that are generally on offer within schools (Daniels et al. 1999). There are many specific types of special needs to include: dyslexia, dyspraxia, **Autistic Spectrum Disorder (ASD)** and **Attention Deficit Hyperactivity Disorder (ADHD)**. Children with special needs will require additional support. The SENCO within a school is there to advise both teachers and teaching assistants on how best to support a pupil with special needs.

Family and care history

It goes without saying that what happens within family life will influence how a child behaves at school. At one extreme a small number of children will for a number of reasons be in the care of the local authority. Sadly, for some children the reasons for being removed from the family are physical or sexual abuse. It is known that many children who are 'looked after' will underachieve and leave school early. The government in trying to address the needs of this group of children have stated that each child in care must have a Personal Educational Plan (PEP).

For children who are living with their parent(s) issues of family bereavement, illness, divorce and general family dynamics will influence their behaviour in the classroom. Common sense tells us that if a child is emotionally unsettled then they will have difficulties settling at school.

Stereotyping and labelling

Stereotyping and labelling involves placing individuals into categories and making assumptions and judgements about these individuals. For example if I said Mr Brown was an accountant you might have an image of what he is like without even meeting him. If I said Miss Smith was a circus trapeze artist you would have a completely different impression. Stereotypes are damaging when they lead to prejudice and discrimination. As a TA, part of your role is to support equal opportunities for all the pupils you work with.

Self-esteem

Self-esteem involves self-evaluation. This evaluation involves a comparison between your **self-image** (the way you see yourself) and your **ideal self** (the way you would like to be). As a TA your role is to help a pupil develop high esteem, that is, help the pupil feel good about who they are.

Age

As an individual progresses through the school system, from pre-school to infants, from juniors to secondary, they change in many ways. Knowing what behaviour is expected from a child, or what behaviour is age-appropriate helps you, the TA, understand the children you are working with. Knowing what is age-appropriate behaviour also makes it easy to identify those children who may benefit from additional support.

Gender

In this case gender refers to how a child acts as a male or female, that is, how masculine or feminine they are. In our society there are said to be sex-role stereotypes. Sex-role stereotypes state the behaviour that is believed to be appropriate for our sex or gender.

Traditional stereotypes such as 'big boys don't cry' or 'girls are not good at maths' can limit the emotional and academic development of pupils. As a TA your role is to discourage stereotypes that limit the development of pupils.

Culture

Culture refers to the learned and shared behaviour of members of a society. Those individuals belonging to the same culture would have similar attitudes, values and beliefs. Subculture refers to those groups, who though sharing many aspects of the mainstream culture, would have distinctive beliefs and values, for example New Age travellers. Ethnocentrism refers to the tendency of judging and evaluating another culture in terms of our own.

Nowadays the United Kingdom is said to be a culturally diverse society. As a TA your role is to promote mutual respect between various cultures and subcultures.

Stages in emotional growth

Erik Erikson (1982) developed a stage theory in regard to emotional growth. At each stage there is a conflict or challenge that needs to be addressed. This conflict can be

Figure 8.3 TAs need to recognise uncharacteristic behaviour

Age	*Psychosocial or emotional conflict*		*Description*
	Resolved positively = emotional growth	*Resolved negatively = emotional immaturity*	
0–1	Trust	Mistrust	Trust is gained through the experience of being able to rely on others. At this stage the infant or small child needs to rely on their parents to provide food, warmth and care. If the child's needs are met the child learns to trust. If the child's needs are not met this legacy of mistrusting others will affect the child's future emotional growth.
1–3	Autonomy	Shame and doubt	Autonomy refers to independence, a sense of being in control of and being able to control what happens to you. At this stage the child must be given the opportunity to assert itself and do things for themselves. If the child experiences constant criticism or is never allowed to try to do things for themselves the child will learn to doubt their abilities and to anticipate failure.
3–6	Initiative	Guilt	At this stage children will develop initiative by being asked to carry out plans. These plans could concern what to paint or what to construct with a set of building blocks. The child while putting their plans into action will also need to respect the rights of others. The child who has in the previous stage learnt to doubt their abilities will find it difficult to try new tasks as they fear failure. As a TA you will need to encourage pupils to have a go.
6–11	Industry	Inferiority	At this stage school age children will need to master academic and social skills in order to feel competent. If they feel they are not as good as their fellow pupils they will start to feel inferior. As a TA you will need to help children to recognise areas that they are good at.
12–20	Identity	Role confusion	Teenagers need to ask themselves questions about the type of person they want to become as an adult. This stage involves dealing with social, and as they mature, sexual relationships. This stage also involves deciding on career goals, for example do they want to go to college or do they want to go to work. What is important at this stage is that the individual pupil really thinks about what they want to do. As a TA you can help them in the thinking process.

Source: Sigelman and Shaffer 1991

resolved positively or negatively. If the outcome is not positive we carry this negativity over, making it more difficult to meet the challenges of the next stage. What is summarised in the tables oppposite and below relates to the stages of emotional growth up to 18 years of age. As a TA your role is to support the pupils you are working with to resolve these conflicts or challenges in a positive manner.

Stages in friendship

Stages in friendship	*How friendships are seen*
Pre-school	Friendships are based on physical aspects. Friends are those who play with you or who are physically near you.
Primary	The key concept here is reciprocal trust. Friends help and support each other. Friends are those you can trust.
Secondary	The key concept here is mutual understanding. Friends understand each other. They confide in each other their innermost thoughts and feelings. Friends comfort each other and forgive each other.
Late adolescence and early adulthood	At this stage there is an awareness that even a very good friendship cannot fill every need. An individual will realise that their friend needs other friends and that the nature of friendships change with time. A good friendship grows and adapts to changes.

Source: Selman 1980; Damon 1983; Berndt 1983

Popularity

In a classroom pupils can be classified into categories reflecting social status. There are children who are

- *popular:* well liked by most children
- *rejected:* rarely liked and often disliked by most children
- *neglected:* children who are neither liked nor disliked but seem to be invisible
- *controversial:* children who are liked by many and disliked by many.

(Coie et al. 1982)

Friendships are important. As a TA you can encourage friendships and friendly behaviour. You will also need to be on the lookout for pupils who seem rejected or neglected and pass this information on to the teacher or SENCO. These children might benefit from social skills training.

Physical milestones

Physical milestones incorporate both gross and fine motor skills. Gross motor skills are the abilities required to control the large muscles of the body. Gross motor skills are involved in walking and running. Fine motor skills describe the smaller more precise motor skills that are involved in handwriting or tying up shoelaces.

As a TA it is important to realise that children will reach these physical milestones at different rates. When a child is considerably delayed in reaching these milestones then there is an issue of concern and this information needs to be passed on to the teacher or the SENCO. The SENCO might raise these concerns with the school nurse.

Age-related abilities

Age	Gross motor skills	Fine motor skills
4–5	• Jump forwards ten times without falling over • Turn somersault • Bounce and catch balls	• Cut on line continuously • Copy a cross and square • Print some capital letters
5–6	• Can walk on a balance beam • Can skate and skip on alternate feet • Can walk on tip-toes	• Cut out simple shapes • Copy a triangle • Copy first name • Colour within lines • Has an adult grasp of pencil • Has a well-established preference for being left or right handed
8–9	• Typically can ride a bike, swim, roller skate, ice skate, and play a variety of sports	

The sort of behaviour patterns that might indicate problems such as child abuse, substance abuse or bullying

Signs and symptoms are detailed in the table on pages 128–9.

In looking for indicators it is important to:

- Recognise that not all children who are experiencing these difficulties will show all these indicators.
- If a child has some of these indicators it does not mean that they will necessarily be experiencing that problem. For example a child may give an improbable explanation for an injury but that does not necessarily mean they are being abused. There may be other explanations. But what these symptoms do indicate is that there is an issue of concern that needs further investigation.
- If you feel that there are issues of concern then you need to follow the school's policies and report your concern to the school's designated **Child Protection Liaison Officer** (**CPLO**).

For example:

Teaching assistant: I work with a Year 4 pupil, Amy, who is a very pretty girl. Amy is a bit on the heavy side and has been teased by the other girls for being fat. Recently Amy has lost a lot of weight. As I also work as a meal-time supervisor I noticed that Amy is just pretending to eat her food and actually is throwing her lunch out everyday. I mentioned this to the teacher as I was concerned about her behaviour and any possible eating disorders.

Teaching assistant: I work with a Year 9 class. I noticed that one of the pupils I supported was extremely tired in class. When I asked him why he seemed reluctant to talk about this. This was not just a one-off situation but had been going on for a few weeks. I mentioned this to the teacher and she said she would look into it. As it turned out the pupil's mother has been in hospital and he has been given a lot of extra responsibilities at home in regard to looking after the younger children.

3.1.2 Support the implementation of strategies to manage pupil behaviour

The specialist advice on behaviour management which is available within the school and how to access this if needed

Managing behaviour in a school calls for teamwork. If you are having difficulty dealing with a pupil then the first person to see is the classroom teacher. The classroom teacher will gain support and advice from the SENCO. In some instances the school will call on advice from outside support agencies, which include the following:

- *The Behaviour Support Team* will be involved with primary schools and work with teachers to support pupils who have particular difficulties in behaviour.
- *The Looked After Children Team* will provide support to children who are in children's homes or foster care. This team will work with the school to implement a Personal Educational Plan that is designed to raise educational standards for these 'at risk' children.
- *The support team for ethnic minority pupils* aims to offer support to schools in regard to working with pupils from ethnic minority backgrounds, supporting bilingual learners, offering guidance on the needs of refugees and asylum seekers and welcoming new arrivals. The support could be in the form of offering practical advice on how pupils can be supported in learning English as an additional language.
- *The traveller education support service* aims to raise awareness and encourage understanding of the social and cultural traditions of this group.
- *The Educational Welfare Service* monitors and promotes regular school attendance. This service will deal with pupils who have problems with attendance.
- *The Educational Psychology Service*, educational psychologists, use knowledge of educational and psychological theory to advise and support schools in dealing with the specific concerns of pupils.

Behaviour support plans

Pupils who have specific issues related to behaviour may have a Behaviour Support Plan or behavioural targets written on an IEP. Later in this chapter we will see an example of a behaviour plan. Simply a behaviour plan states the goal or target, in terms of desired behaviour the pupil should be working towards. In order to meet the target certain *strategies* are put into place and then after a certain time all those concerned meet to discuss whether the strategies have been successful and the targets have been met.

The key to having a successful behaviour plan is devising suitable targets. According to current terminology these targets need to be SMART, that is, targets need to be:

- *Specific:* targets need to describe the behaviour the pupil is aiming for in clear and precise terms. After reading the target you should fully understand what it is that the pupil is working towards.
- *Measurable:* targets take into account the number of times a behaviour occurs, the frequency, and how long the behaviour goes on for, the duration. The behaviour plan should mention what the behaviour was like to begin with and what it is hoped that the behaviour will be like by the review session.
- *Achievable:* targets set in the behaviour plan should be achievable for the pupil.
- *Relevant:* targets need to be related to the specific needs of the pupil.
- *Time-limited:* a realistic time is given for the pupil to achieve the target.

Signs and symptoms

Neglect	*Child abuse (physical/sexual)*	*Bullying*	*Depression*	*Eating disorder*	*Drug or substance abuse*
• Clothes are not clean (e.g. child soiled themselves, child given a clean change of clothes at school, took soiled clothes home and returned to school next day wearing these soiled clothes)	• Unexplained injuries • Improbable excuses for injuries • Wearing clothes to hide injuries • Refusal to undress for PE	• The victim may become withdrawn	• Talk of feeling unhappy, miserable, lonely • May seem tearful, moody, irritable, easily upset • In extreme circum-stances may talk of wishing to die	• Eating too much or too little or using harmful ways to reduce weight	• Change in sleeping patterns • Changes in personality • Sudden mood swings
• Poor hygiene (e.g. other children complain of child smelling, persistent and chronic infestations of head lice)	• Being knowledgeable of sexual activity in a way that is inappropriate for the child's age reflected in child's behaviour to other children, in what they say to other children, in what they draw	• The pupil may suddenly decide not to come to school	• May feel guilty • May blame themselves for everything	• Eating too few calories • Using slimming pills or laxatives to control weight gain • Binge eating following by self-induced vomiting • Excessive exercise to reduce weight	• Lack of personal hygiene • No energy or interest in activities • Lack of interest in normal social life

• Constant hunger • Child persistently steals food from other children's lunch boxes	• Being isolated and withdrawn • Difficulties in concentrating • Difficulties in trusting others	• The pupil's academic work may decline	• Changes in behaviour • May stop caring about their appearance • May stop eating or eat more • May stop seeing their friends or participating in social activities	• Thinking they are too fat when they are clearly under-weight • Obsessive about weight and food • Possible depression, difficulties in sleeping	• Unexpected aggression • Disappearance of money, complain of shortage of cash
• Constantly tired (for example falling asleep at desk)	• Sudden change in personality • Suddenly behaving like a much younger child	• The pupil may begin to display negative behaviour	• May seem tired at school have difficulties in concentrating		
• Untreated medical problems (child comes to school when clearly unwell)	• Self-destructive • Suicide attempts • Aggressive to others • Running away				
• Problems with making friends with other children	• Medical complaints (sexual abuse – pain or itching in genital region) • Fearful of medical examinations				

As a TA you need to know:

- The behaviour targets of any pupils you are working with
- The strategies to use with these pupils to help them meet their targets
- Whom to talk to regarding the pupil's progress

An example of a Behaviour Support Plan can be found on page 134.

Sorts of situations which could present a risk to you or others' safety and strategies for diverting or defusing potential flash points

The school has a duty to safeguard the behaviour of all pupils. There are situations, which could present risks. Some of these risks are to do with health and safety and have been covered elsewhere in this book (see page 138). Some risks come about as a result of extremely challenging and aggressive behaviour of pupils. For example what do you do if two pupils are fighting? What do you do if these are secondary pupils and they are considerably bigger than you? What do you do if a pupil picks up a chair and threatens to throw it at the other pupils?

- In the first place it is important to know your school's policy in regard to extreme behaviour and reasonable physical restraint.
- Remember you are part of a team. In extreme situations there are procedures to follow. Schools will often have a procedure where you can call for assistance. As a TA you need to know this procedure.
- Preventive measures are always best! If you have been working with a pupil who has extremely challenging behaviour you may be able to pick up on the warning signs such as a change in their body language. A noisy pupil may all of a sudden become quiet; a quiet pupil may become noisy. The pupil's face may redden; they may clench their fists. The key is to intervene early and remove them to a quiet place where they can calm down.
- If a pupil is very aggressive the advice is to ensure the other pupils' safety and your own, by moving out of harm's way. In terms of reacting to the pupil displaying the challenging behaviour remain calm and talk in a soothing voice.

Checklist

✔ I am familiar with school policies regarding behaviour.
✔ I encourage pupils to remember the rules.
✔ I encourage pupils to think about how their behaviour affects other pupils.
✔ I encourage pupils to think about choices and consequences.
✔ If a reprimand is necessary, I think about how I am going to give the reprimand.
✔ I know the behaviour targets of the students I am working with.
✔ I praise the students.
✔ I remember that managing behaviour involves teamwork.

MEETING PERFORMANCE INDICATORS

3.1.1 Promote school policies with regard to pupil behaviour

Setting the scene

At the start of the day Mrs Goldbottom, the class teacher, reviews the class behaviour strategies with Miranda – Mrs Goldbottom states there are a few pupils in this class who can be challenging. At home that evening before writing up the session as a personal account, Miranda reviews *some* of the performance indicators she should cover.

Unit 3.1.1 Promote school policies with regard to pupil behaviour

Performance indicator	*Scope*
(4) Recognise when pupil behaviour conflicts with school policy.	(a) Behaviour Policy (b) On bullying (c) On use of language (d) On the treatment of other pupils and adults in school (e) For equal opportunities (f) On movement within the school, school grounds and immediate vicinity of the school (g) For access to, and use of, school facilities and equipment
(5) Respond promptly to inappropriate behaviour in line with your role and level of responsibility.	
(6) Remind pupils of school policies on behaviour in a calm and appropriate manner using language that they can understand and relate to.	(a) Behaviour Policy (b) On bullying (c) On use of language (d) On the treatment of other pupils and adults in school (e) For equal opportunities (f) On movement within the school, school grounds and immediate vicinity of the school. (g) For access to, and use of, school facilities and equipment

Unit 3.1.2 Support the implementation of strategies to manage pupil behaviour

Performance indicators	*Scope*
(1) Confirm your understanding of the strategies to be used to manage pupil behaviour.	(a) For use with individual pupils (b) For use with groups of pupils (c) For use with the whole class
(2) Are consistent and effective in implementing the agreed strategies.	(a) For use with individual pupils (b) For use with groups of pupils (c) For use with the whole class
(3) Recognise and respond appropriately to risks to yourself and/or others during episodes of challenging behaviour.	

(4) Promptly report any problems in implementing the agreed strategies to the teacher.

(a) For use with individual pupils
(b) For use with groups of pupils
(c) For use with the whole class

Personal Account

Name: Miranda Appleton
Date: 25 January 2006
Activity: Year 3 class participating in a numeracy session

Who was involved

I was working with a small group of pupils – Sharon, Michael, Kylie, David, Jason and Sinead. This group struggles with numeracy.

Confirm your understanding of the strategies to be used to manage pupil behaviour (3.1.2 1ab)

Before the numeracy session commenced I had a quick chat with the teacher regarding the lesson objectives and about Sharon. Sharon has been having difficulties in getting on with the other children in the class. The teacher and I talked about these difficulties and the teacher talked about ways of working with Sharon. Sharon needed to be reminded of the class rules and praised when she keeps to the rules. We also reviewed class strategies regarding behaviour for groups.

Mrs G in the session talked about different ways that you can add up. When the class divided for group work I was working with the Yellow Group. The group had to divide into pairs and each had a set of dice. They had to throw the dice and write the numbers down. Then they had to add the numbers together.

Are consistent and effective in implementing agreed policies

I began the group session by reminding the pupils of expected behaviour; that they had to do their work, take turns rolling the dice and to listen to what each other said (3.1.2 2b). For the first five minutes all the children were working well and I told them about how impressed I was with their behaviour (3.1.1 4a).

Recognise when pupils' behaviour conflicts with school policy

Respond promptly to inappropriate behaviour in line with your role and level of responsibility

Well shortly after that Sharon grabbed David's pencil and would not give it back. I reminded Sharon that one of the class rules was to share equipment and that I expected her to follow this. I asked her what she should do? Sharon gave the pencil back and said sorry. I praised her for this (3.1.1 4ag 1g).

A few minutes later David complained that Sharon was not letting him have a turn at throwing the dice. I again reminded Sharon of the class rules. Sharon gave David the dice, but then Sharon grabbed the dice from the other group. I asked Sharon what did she think she was doing. Sharon said that she did not have to listen to me and that she didn't want to do the work anyway.

Well, I had reminded Sharon about appropriate behaviour twice before but these reminders did not seem to work. The fact that Sharon was rude to me was the last straw. I reported the behaviour to the teacher. Mrs Goldbottom told Sharon that her behaviour was out of order and that she would not be going out to break. Sharon apologised to me for being rude (3.1.1 5ag 8).

Evaluation

I think I was right to inform the teacher regarding Sharon's behaviour. To begin with Sharon was working – but then her behaviour fell apart. Thinking about it I realised that she started being disruptive when we started to use the dice with the larger numbers. Perhaps Sharon was finding the work too difficult and felt that she needed to play up to get out of doing the work. I mentioned this to Mrs G.

Teacher's comments

I was aware of the problems Miranda was having with the Yellow Group. Miranda used a number of strategies that we had talked about. Miranda acted appropriately in this situation by informing me of Sharon's consistent misbehaviour. Miranda's observation of perhaps Sharon having difficulty with the larger numbers was a valid one and in future perhaps Miranda can suggest that they work through the difficult sums together.

I certify that this is a true statement of what occurred.

Teacher's signature	Name (printed and role)
R. Goldbottom	Rosaline Goldbottom Year 3 Class Teacher

Miranda when handing in this evidence includes a short note to her assessor Terrie.

Dear Terrie

I am pleased with what I have written and with the teacher's comments. I am a bit concerned with how I am going to meet all the other indicators. I know I am going to have problems with '*Recognise and respond appropriately to risks to yourself/and/or others during episodes of challenging behaviour*'.

I work in a primary school and on the whole the children are very good. Nothing ever dramatic happens – nothing like what the girls from the secondary school behaviour unit talk about.

xxx

Miranda

Assessor's comments

Miranda, this personal account is very good evidence. The way you structured your account using performance indicators as headings was very helpful. Also well done for including the number references for the performance indicators you have covered. Remember there are other ways of gathering evidence for this unit, witness statements, incident report forms and annotated behaviour plans. Also remember that NVQs are designed to adapt to the varying teaching environments that TAs work in. What is challenging behaviour really depends on the pupils you work with. What is challenging behaviour in a primary school will not necessarily be the same as challenging behaviour in a secondary school. However, saying that, it is important to know the school policies in regarding handling very serious incidents of challenging behaviour – should anything like that ever happen.

Signed: Terrie Cole

Terrie Cole
NVQ Assessor

Anywhere Primary

Behaviour Plan
Name: JS
Area of concern:
Running out of the classroom

This is a copy of a behaviour plan for a pupil I support. This tells me the strategies I should use.

Year Group: 1
Class Teacher: Lizzie Stubbs — Review date: March 2006
Support by: Miranda Appleton — Support began: Oct. 2005

Targets to be achieved	*Achievement criteria*	*Possible resources or techniques*	*Possible class strategies*	*Ideas for teaching assistant*	*Outcome*
To reduce running out of the classroom behaviour by 50%	If achieves 5 incidents a week (down from 10 incidents) in three weeks	Use of special box of rewards for remaining in class	Remind him of appropriate behaviour Reward him for appropriate behaviour	In time alone talk about appropriate behaviour Keep records	Met achievement criteria

Case study

I have been working with JS for over six months now. JS has a behaviour plan. One of the difficulties JS has is with running out of the classroom. The strategies that are used are to remind J at the beginning of the day of the need to stay in the class. It was suggested that J has a special box of rewards. In this box are special activities and games he has chosen. If he stays in the class at the end of the day he can spend 15 minutes with me playing his special games. J really enjoys this. As I have worked with J for over six months I am very good at realising when he is about to run out of the classroom. It is at that point I go over to him and point out his special box. Pointing out his special box is usually enough to keep him focused. I keep the teacher informed on a day-to-day basis regarding J's behaviour.

Teacher's comments

Miranda has worked very hard at developing a positive relationship with JS and her work with him has helped him to accept classroom boundaries.

Lizzie Stubbs Class Teacher March 2006

Anywhere Primary

Incident Report Form
Pupil: JS
Date: 5 December 2005

After lunch J was finding it difficult to settle in class. Today was a lovely day and J wanted to stay out in the playground. When Mrs S (supply teacher) started science group work J got up from his seat. Another pupil S told him to sit down. J screamed at this pupil. I positioned myself between J and the other pupil. At this point J made a mad dash. I spent 20 minutes in the hall trying to coax J back into class. Due to his behaviour Mrs S made J spend afternoon break doing work. J was very tearful for rest of the day. Perhaps when it is a nice day we could suggest that if he behaves we could do some special games outside.

M. Appleton

Assessor's comments

Miranda

This is good hard evidence. Well done for annotating your behaviour plan. A few lines are often all that you need.

Also well done for remembering the need for confidentiality.

The case study and incident report form provide good evidence for providing feedback to the teacher on progress made by any pupils with a Behaviour Support Plan and making suggestions of improving behaviour management strategies.

J's behaviour may not be quite as dramatic as the tales from the secondary behaviour unit – but his behaviour is challenging. The fact that you positioned yourself between J and the other pupil showed that you recognised and responded to potential risks to yourself and others.

Signed: Terrie Cole

Terrie Cole
NVQ Assessor

Nicola, our secondary TA, also hands in evidence to the assessor.

Witness Statement

Date: 20 March 2006
School: Wherever Secondary

Nicola was in the vicinity of the school office as the pupils were going out for break. I observed D.S. and T.W. having what looked like a verbal argument. D.S. at that point lost control and started ripping artwork off the wall, throwing them to the ground and stamping on them, screaming. I quickly made sure that all the other pupils left the area.

As Nicola was nearest to D.S. and has spent considerable hours supporting D.S., Nicola quickly moved behind D.S. and started to quietly whisper to him. At this point D.S. started to cry. Nicola put her arms around D.S. and quickly moved him to a quiet room near by.

Nicola handled this episode in a professional manner following school guidelines regarding challenging behaviour.

I commend Nicola for her quick and sensitive action.

Malcolm Marsh Head of Year

Assessor's comments

Nicola

A very difficult situation that was sensitively handled. Well done!

Signed: Terrie Cole

Terrie Cole

NVQ Assessor

Chapter 9

Unit 3.10 Support the maintenance of pupil safety and security

In this unit there are two elements:

3.10.1 Contribute to the maintenance of a safe and secure learning environment
3.10.2 Minimise the risks arising from health emergencies

KNOWLEDGE BASE

3.10.1 Contribute to the maintenance of a safe and secure learning environment

Every member of staff employed in a school has, as a primary duty, to give consideration to the health and safety of both the pupils and the other staff. It is everyone's responsibility to ensure that the school environment is both safe and secure for all the community. In this context the school environment includes all buildings, the grounds of the school and out-of-school trips and visits.

Some members of staff have designated responsibilities and you, as a teaching assistant, need to know which members of staff these are. You need to be familiar with your general responsibility and who to turn to when the need arises. If there is an accident in class, for instance, and a pupil is injured, you should immediately know where to summon help.

School policies and procedures with regard to health and safety, waste disposal and security

Health and Safety Policy

Each school by law has to have a Health and Safety Policy in place which is reviewed annually by governors and staff (see also pages 15 and 139–144). This should have been given to you as part of your induction. Included in this policy should be a list of staff members qualified in first aid, some of whom will have completed the 'First Aid at Work' course.

For more details on the statutory duties relating to schools see the information regarding the Health and Safety at Work Act 1974, the Children Acts 1989 and 2004, the Management of Health and Safety Regulations 1992, the Disability

Discrimination Acts 1995 and 2005 and the Special Educational Needs and Disability Act (SENDA) 2001 in Chapter 13.

Local authority policies

Each school will also need to comply with policies and procedures drawn up by their local authorities.

Specific responsibilities

Ultimately it is the Board of Governors who has the legal responsibility for health and safety within the school. However, the school's policy should outline the specific responsibilities of members of staff who support them in this – the head teacher, the school's Health and Safety Officer, the caretaker, office staff, class teachers, non-teaching staff, mealtime supervisors, cleaners and crossing patrols.

Class teachers and teaching assistants

Class teachers are responsible both for the safety of their learning environment and for the children in their care. This begins with the legal responsibility to take registers at the start of each morning and each afternoon in compliance with school procedures. It is a legal requirement of every school to know which pupils are present in the building at any one time.

Every class teacher and teaching assistant working with them needs to know the exact procedures to be employed in their learning environment in the event of an accident or emergency. This includes evacuating the building in the event of a fire or bomb scare. They also need to be aware of and observe standards of health and safety as they apply to their learning environment. This includes cables safely secured, exits free from obstruction, tables and chairs safe to sit on and use as well as potentially dangerous equipments and materials, such as scissors and glues, safely and securely stored when not in use and adequately supervised when they are in use.

Limits of responsibility

Every member of staff also needs to know the limits of their responsibility – for instance, they should not attempt to repair damaged electrical or electronic goods. This should be reported to the appropriate person and dealt with according to the school's policy and procedures. No member of staff should bring their own electric or electronic equipment into school for pupils to use – everything used by pupils must first be checked for safety by local authority officers.

First aid

First aid should be rendered to staff or pupils alike only as far as knowledge and skill permit. Where there is blood or other bodily fluids involved, disposable gloves must be worn. If someone is sick, this must be covered with approved disinfectant and the appropriate person called for to clean it up. In the event of accidents or injuries, school procedures must be followed at all times. Only those members of staff with appropriate qualifications, training and recognition are to administer medication.

Security

Schools are not prisons, but unfortunately we live in days when they must be secure. The idea is not to keep pupils and staff in, but to keep unwanted people out. Each school will have its own system of external and internal security. You need to be familiar with this and maintain the relevant procedures (see Figure 9.1).

Most schools operate some system of identifying visitors – normally a badge. Every member of staff has a responsibility to challenge anyone on the premises they do not recognise who is not wearing such an identification.

Road safety

While travel to and from the school is the responsibility of parents and carers rather than school staff, the school has a duty to teach and train the pupils in road safety. Alongside the class teacher, you have a responsibility to ensure that pupils in your care,

Figure 9.1 Security is important

particularly in the younger years, know how to cross roads and use the pavements safely. The school may have a policy on using bicycles, skateboards or roller blades to come to school. You must be familiar with this and reinforce school procedures whenever the occasion arises.

Off-site activities

The school Health and Safety Policy will also relate to off-site activities, stating the level of pupil–teacher ratio needed for particular ages and activities. The policy may also make reference to visitors and animals on site and to any potentially hazardous parts of the school environment such as a pond.

Your legal duties for health and safety in the workplace as required by relevant Health and Safety at Work legislation

As well as the general legislation outlined above, there are specific duties required of you if you are responsible for pupils.

Don't strain yourself or your children

You are required not to try to move objects beyond your strength (see Figure 9.2). Where you have children under your direct supervision, it is your responsibility to instruct them in how to safely move equipment, should that be needed. They should never be allowed to move awkward objects such as pianos or televisions.

Don't clutter the doors or corridors

You are required to ensure all exits and access points to the learning environment within which you are working are clear and free from obstruction.

Figure 9.2 Don't strain yourself

Don't let your children go with just anybody

You must follow school procedures when allowing pupils to leave the learning environment, which will vary according to their age. At Key Stage 1, for instance, it will probably be the case that you can release pupils only into the direct care of a parent or a recognised person at the end of the day.

Don't drop rubbish

All waste products must be disposed of safely in line with school procedures. If you are cooking, for instance, you are responsible for the disposal of food waste and for cleaning the equipment both before and after use.

Your responsibilities for health, safety and security as defined in your job description

If teaching assistants are required to take the register either as part of their regular duties or only occasionally as situations dictate, then they should be fully trained in this and operate under the supervision of a class teacher.

If your duties include that of accompanying teachers and pupils on off-site visits and activities you should be clear as to what your responsibilities are. If you drive a minibus you will need to have received appropriate training and gained a recognised qualification. You may be asked to keep a register of small groups of children, collect pocket money, medicines etc. You may also be asked to collate information regarding medications and potential illnesses of pupils going on the trip, particularly if the trip is over a number of days. In order to do this you may, for instance, be asked to collect all medical forms from parents, read through them and make a list of those pupils with identified medical needs. This list will need to be given to the school office and to the teachers responsible for the trip.

As a teaching assistant you may be asked to perform specific functions in respect to emergency procedures, for instance, checking the toilets or other non-teaching areas in the event of evacuation of the building. This should be agreed with you beforehand, written into your job description and adequate training and preparation given to you.

Whatever you are asked to do, this should be an agreed part of your job description and should be planned with you and with all relevant members of staff beforehand. This will include discussion with the school's Health and Safety Officer to ensure all legal requirements are being met.

Legal and school requirements for child protection and your role and responsibilities in relation to this

The school will have a Child Protection Liaison Officer (CPLO). However, every member of staff has a specific responsibility regarding child protection. You need to be familiar with the school's Child Protection Policy which should have been given to you as part of your induction package.

Your responsibility is to report any suspicions to the relevant person – normally the class teacher you are working with, but it may be the SENCO or the CPLO directly. Suspicions may be aroused by such things as unusual changes in a child's manner or behaviour (such as being excessively withdrawn or acting out-of-character), by physical marks which cannot be accounted for by the normal 'wear and tear' which children experience, or by actual disclosure.

You have a legal duty to report any concerns. It is not up to you to make a judgement as to whether the situation constitutes child protection or not. You must be aware of and follow school policy and procedure very carefully and explicitly as any deviation may prejudice further investigation.

You are not allowed to ask leading or probing questions. You must report children's actual words and not put words into their mouths. You must keep to the time limits within which reports must be made such as reporting on the same day that a disclosure is made.

Health, safety and security risks which may occur (for self, others and the environment) and the appropriate action to take when they do

Awareness of risk is often largely a matter of common sense; but it does involve being alert to potential hazards. You should always be on the lookout for things which could be dangerous. It is all too easy to become used to bags strewn on the floor, coats lying under hooks rather than being hung up, carpets rucked up rather then being flat. Every member of staff has a responsibility to minimise such risks.

The responsible person to whom to report health and safety matters

You have a legal obligation to report any hazards to the relevant person. This will vary from school to school, but most likely will involve some kind of system for either directly reporting to the school's Health and Safety Officer or for writing down concerns in a book which is looked at daily by the caretaker or Health and Safety Officer. No member of staff can say, 'It's somebody else's job, I'm too busy to do anything about it'.

The scope of equipment and materials used within the learning environment, any risks to safety associated with their use, and, where part of your job role, how to use them correctly and safely to minimise risk

Some materials and equipment obviously carry more risk than others. You will need to be alert to this and, where appropriate, receive training in the use of such equipment.

Methods of storing different equipment and materials safely and securely

All equipment should be stored appropriately and safely. Even an untidy cupboard could be breaking health and safety regulations if material in it is stored in such a way that it could fall out and injure the person opening the doors.

The reasons for providing information on your whereabouts and the school procedures for doing this

If there is a fire or any other emergency, those with responsibility for evacuating the building or for dealing with the emergency need to know where you are. It is not enough that they should know you are in the building somewhere. In a small primary school this may not be so much of an issue as it is in a secondary school with over a thousand pupils, where large numbers of staff are possibly spread between several buildings.

You need to become familiar with school procedures for noting your whereabouts and follow them. It may seem picky, but it is vital that an appropriate response can be made to an emergency.

The appropriate action to take for different emergencies such as fire, evacuation of buildings, bomb scares and intruder(s)

As a teaching assistant you should take part in the regular evacuation drills held by the school. This can be an issue if you work only part time. If it transpires that such drills took place when you were not in school and you therefore missed them, you should talk with the person responsible to ensure that the next drill occurs at a time when you can participate. You should be made familiar with school policies regarding emergencies – if you are unsure, ask.

The relationship of fire extinguisher/blanket to fire type (electrical, chemical, combustible material)

Fires require fuel, heat and oxygen to burn. Extinguishers remove heat and oxygen and so deprive the fuel of the ability to burn. It is important therefore to use the appropriate type of extinguisher when tackling different types of fire. If, for instance, you use water on an electrical or chemical fire, you will make matters considerably worse.

Wood, paper and textile fires can be tackled with water. Foam can tackle these fires as well as fires of petrol, oil, fats and paints. Powder or carbon dioxide extinguishers need to be used on gas and electrical fires. A fire blanket should be used to smother flames actually on a person's clothing. It is important that extinguishers are applied thoroughly to ensure the core of the fire and not just the surface is dealt with.

Generally speaking, however, your responsibility will be to participate in the evacuation of the building rather than attempt to put out a fire.

Checklist

- ✔ I am familiar with my school's Health and Safety Policy and procedures.
- ✔ I am aware of my own responsibilities to maintain the safety and security of the school community.
- ✔ I am aware of the limits of my responsibilities and role and know who to call on if I need support.
- ✔ I am familiar with my school's Child Protection Policy and procedures.
- ✔ I am familiar with my school's emergency procedures and have participated in practice fire drills.

3.10.2 Minimise the risks arising from health emergencies

The signs and symptoms of the different emergency conditions and how these may differ in relation to an individual's age and for people from different ethnic groups (see page 146)

In all instances, the probability is that the younger the child, the more distressing it is probably going to be for the pupil. Older children are more likely to be able to understand what is happening, whereas younger ones may need a good deal of reassurance.

The importance and purpose of calling assistance immediately

In any emergency, time is of the essence. In some situations it might literally be a case of life or death. It is therefore vital to call for the appropriate help immediately. This means each school must have in place tried and tested procedures for summoning help. It is important that the correct person is called for because they will know exactly how to respond and what to do. It is not sufficient for willing people to 'have a go' at providing support. Calling for assistance is not a sign of weakness, but of wisdom and care for the person or persons at risk.

Who the designated First Aider is within the setting and how to contact him or her in an emergency

Schools should communicate to all staff information about the designated First Aiders – who they are and how they can be reached at any moment in the day. You need to know who to go to and how to reach them if an emergency were to happen. It is too late to find out as the emergency is occurring. This should also apply if you are driving a school minibus. You should always carry an active mobile phone to be able to contact appropriate staff in an emergency.

The actions which you should start to take, and those things which you should not do, for each of the emergencies listed in the scope of this standard

If you are not a trained First Aider the actions you should take are restricted to summoning help and providing reassurance to the person concerned unless it is absolutely necessary. You should avoid moving the person unless it is essential. The following suggestions about how to respond to specific emergencies are only outlines and *should not be regarded as full instructions* (see page 148).

Placing a person in the recovery position

Putting an unconscious person into the recovery position will prevent them choking on blood, vomit or saliva. You should place an unconscious person into the recovery position unless they have injured their head, neck or spine.

Emergency	*Signs and symptoms*
Severe bleeding	Minor grazes would not count as a health emergency, but bleeding which is severe and continuous would – either the initial amount of blood loss or the continuing loss of blood would constitute an emergency – both may result in the patient feeling faint
Cardiac arrest	Vice-like chest pain, spreading to one or both arms; difficulty breathing; discomfort in the upper abdomen region; fainting; collapse; pale skin and blue lips; pulse gains in speed, then weakens; sweating
Shock	Rapid pulse; pale, cold clammy skin; sweating; grey-blue skin later; weakness and giddiness; nausea or thirst; rapid, shallow breathing; weak pulse
Anaphylactic shock	Anxiety; red, blotchy skin; tongue and throat swells; eyes become puffy; breathing becomes laboured, possibly with wheezing and gasping for air; signs of shock
Faints or loss of consciousness	Body slumps; pulse rate immediately slows but should pick up soon; skin becomes pale; sweating
Epileptic seizure	Suddenly loses consciousness; goes rigid and back arches; convulsive movements as muscles seize; muscles relax; there may be fever, twitching of the face, holding of the breath, drooling at the mouth
Choking and difficulty with breathing	Difficulty in breathing; coughing; distress; flushed face and neck; uttering strange noises or making no sound at all; blue-grey skin later – could lose consciousness
Asthma attack	Difficulty in breathing; may be wheezing; difficulty in speaking; grey-blue skin; exhaustion and possible loss of consciousness
Falls	Potential and actual fractures – distortion, swelling and bruising at the site of the injury; pain; difficulty in moving the injured part; there may be bending, twisting or shortening of a limb, there may even be a wound with a bone sticking out
Burns and scalds	Red skin; pain in the area of the burn of scald; skin swells and blisters
Poisoning	Vomiting that may have traces of blood in it; consciousness impaired; pain or burning sensation in the gut
Electrocution	Collapse; loss of consciousness; breathing becomes difficult or even stops; heartbeat may stop; there may be burns where the electricity enters the body and where it exits the body to go to 'earth'; there may be muscular spasms indicating the person is electrically 'charged'
Substance abuse	Similar to poison; hallucinations; loss of memory or rational thought; random or slurred speech; extreme lethargy or excessive activity

1. Kneel down next to the patient and turn their head towards you, lifting it back to open the windpipe.
2. Take the near arm and lay it straight along their side then take the other arm and place it across their chest.
3. Place the ankle further away from you over the near ankle.
4. Keep holding the head with one hand, take the patient's clothing at the hip in the other hand and turn them onto their front by pulling towards you, support them with your knees.
5. Lift the patient's chin forward to keep the windpipe open.
6. Take the arm and leg nearest to you and bend them, pull the other arm out from under the body, keeping the palm up.

Any religious or cultural restrictions on the actions to be taken in response to a health emergency

In any emergency the prime concern will be the safety of the patient and those around them. However, there may be cultural factors to be borne in mind, such as loosening clothing, particularly headwear. There may also be regulations about the type of washing pupils are allowed to perform. Such issues should be agreed with parents before any emergency occurs and this information communicated to all staff.

Your own capabilities to deal with an emergency and the reasons why actions beyond your own capabilities may further endanger life

- *Do no more than you have been trained to do.* Never take matters into your own hands. Always call for those with the training and the responsibility.
- *If you do go beyond your own capabilities you may seriously endanger the person you are trying to help.* Good intentions are not enough. Knowledge is the issue. It may be, for instance, that you instinctively want to give a drink to someone in shock, but this may make the situation worse.

Potential health risks to others from an emergency, such as contamination from blood and other body products

If there is severe bleeding there can be risk of infection – HIV or hepatitis. Any actual sickness must also be treated circumspectly. In these instances you should touch the pupil only when wearing disposable gloves.

How health emergencies might affect others in the vicinity and ways of supporting them effectively once the initial danger is passed

Children who have witnessed the emergency may be distressed and even traumatised; so might members of staff, including yourself. Once the initial danger has passed it is important *not* to carry on as if nothing had happened. The responsible members of staff should ensure that all involved, pupils and staff alike, have the opportunity to talk about the situation and have space to be quiet and respond as they want to.

Emergency	*Responses*
Severe bleeding	The flow of blood needs to be stemmed as soon as possible. This is best achieved by applying pressure to the wound for ten minutes if there is nothing within it. By then the appropriate person should have arrived and they will take over. If there is a foreign body in the wound, this should not be removed but pressure should be placed around it without putting pressure on the object itself.
Cardiac arrest	If the patient is unconscious, place in the recovery position; if he or she is conscious have them half sit up, supporting them with cushions. Do not give them anything to eat or drink.
Shock or anaphylactic shock	The victim should be lain down and any tight clothing loosened, particularly at the neck to help with breathing. If possible, raise the legs higher than the head and keep the victim warm. Do not give them anything to eat or drink.
Faints or loss of consciousness	If someone complains of feeling faint, sit them down and put their head between their knees. If they do faint, lay them on their back and raise their legs so the blood flow is increased to the brain. Tight clothing must be loosened to help with breathing.
Epileptic seizure	The patient must not be moved or restrained; any furniture or other people near them must be moved out of the way to prevent injury. Something soft should be placed under the patient's head if that is possible.
Choking and difficulty with breathing	If there is something actually choking the patient, encourage them to cough. If that does not work, bend them over with their head lower than the chest and slap them five times between the shoulder blades with the flat of your hand.
Asthma attack	Provide reassurance and administer medication (inhaler); possibly giving two doses. Encourage the casualty to breathe slowly. Call for an ambulance if the inhaler has not taken effect after five minutes.
Falls	All suspected fractures must be treated as actual fractures. The casualty must not be moved but a qualified first aider called for immediately. The casualty must be made as comfortable as possible without moving the injured limb.
Burns and scalds	The affected area needs to be cooled with cold water, any clothes attached to the wound must not be removed.
Poisoning	If possible, find out what the victim has swallowed and inform the medical team when they arrive. You should provide reassurance to the patient and watch for them becoming unconscious. Do not try and make them sick.
Electrocution	The source of electricity needs to be cut off, preferably by removing the plug from the socket. You should not touch the victim unless it is absolutely necessary. If you have to move them to remove them from the electrical source, stand on dry insulating material, such as paper or wood, and push the person away using an insulated item such as a stick or a chair. Once the person has been disconnected from the electricity source, place them in the recovery position.
Substance abuse	If you can, find out what they have taken and inform the medical team when they arrive. Do not try to make the patient sick. Provide verbal reassurance and comfort to the patient. Place them in the recovery position if they become unconscious.

Legislative requirements for completing records of accidents and emergencies

The law states that every member of staff in a school must act like a 'prudent parent' in the event of an emergency. Any complaint of illness or hurt must be taken seriously. Minor injuries may be treated by suitably trained staff, but a record must be kept in the school accident log. Any injury to a child's head, however caused, must result in the child being given a note to that effect. If there is anything more than a minor bump the parents or carers must be informed immediately.

As soon as possible after any incident the illness, injury or accident must be fully reported and accurately written up in the appropriate log book. Each school will have their own procedures, but in primary schools such records are likely to be kept and collated in the school office.

Where incidents are more serious the local authority should be notified – the school administration staff will know who to contact.

Checklist

- ✔ I can recognise the symptoms of a range of health emergencies in pupils.
- ✔ I know how to respond to health emergencies in pupils, particularly who to call on for assistance.
- ✔ I have practised placing a person in the recovery position.
- ✔ I am aware of my own capabilities in responding to a health emergency and when I need to call for assistance.
- ✔ I am able to protect myself and to support others in the event of a health emergency.

MEETING PERFORMANCE INDICATORS

3.10.1 Contribute to the maintenance of a safe and secure learning environment

Setting the scene – 1

Miranda is supporting a Year 4 teacher in a design and technology (DT) lesson. Half of a Year 6 class has swapped with half of a Year 4 class, so that there are two classes of mixed years 4 and 6 with equal numbers of each. The Year 4 pupils are to make a wooden maze using a 10 cm square hardboard base, balsa wood spars for the sides and walls of the maze, a small ball bearing to place within the maze and a clear plastic covering. The pupils need to plan their maze, draw it onto the base, cut the appropriate lengths of spars, glue them on to the base using a glue gun, place the ball bearing in the maze and finally tack the plastic covering over the whole piece using drawing pins. The Year 6 pupils have the opportunity to support younger pupils. It is hoped that the older pupils will act as role models as well as instructors for the younger ones.

Setting the scene – 2

There is a planned fire drill while Miranda is working with a group of six Year 2 pupils in a playground away from the class, not within sight of the class teacher. She is overseeing a science activity – investigating 'floating and sinking' using various items in a tank of water.

Writing personal accounts: covering performance indicators

When writing up what she has seen and done, Miranda makes reference to the following performance indicators.

Unit 3.10.1 Contribute to the maintenance of a safe and secure learning environment

Performance indicators	*Scope*
(1) Comply with legal and organisational requirements for maintaining the health, safety and security of yourself and *others* in the learning *environment*.	Scope of *others* (a) Pupils, including any with special educational needs Scope of *environment* (a) The classroom (b) Other areas within the school
(2) Correctly identify any *risks* to the health, safety or security of yourself and *others* and take *appropriate action* to minimise the *risks*.	Scope of *risks* Risks resulting from: (a) The use and maintenance of equipment (b) The use of materials or substances (c) Unsafe behaviour (d) Accidental breakages and spillages Scope of *appropriate action* (a) Taking actions consistent with your role and responsibilities (b) Reporting to the person responsible for health and safety in the setting
(3) Maintain the learning *environment* as safe and free from hazards as possible during work activities.	
(4) Use equipment and materials in a correct, safe manner consistent with current legal and organisational requirements.	
(5) Store equipment and materials safely and securely when not in use.	
(6) Dispose of waste and spillage without delay in a safe manner and place.	
(7) Take *appropriate action* to minimise health, safety and security *risks* which arise during work activities.	
(8) Ensure that accurate information regarding own whereabouts is maintained so that immediate contact can be made should this be necessary.	
(9) Implement appropriate safety procedures without delay in an *emergency*.	Scope of *emergencies* (a) Fire (b) Evacuation of buildings

Personal Account

Name: Miranda Appleton
Date: 30 March 2006
3.10.1 Contribute to the maintenance of a safe and secure learning environment

Y4 Design and Technology lesson

Risk assessment

In line with the school's Health and Safety Policy, which in turn is shaped by national legislation such as the Health and Safety at Work Act 1974 and *Every Child Matters*, the teacher (Mr Canning) and myself undertook a risk assessment several days before the lesson was due to take place. We discussed the areas of hazard which were likely to be encountered by the pupils – the use of small saws which have sharp blades, the use of glue guns which require attachment to electric sockets and which grow hot, small ball bearings which could be thrown, slipped on or even swallowed.

We agreed that having fifteen Year 6 pupils reduced the danger as each one was to be paired with a Year 4 pupil with a specific remit to look after their safety. This meant that, in a class of thirty pupils, only fifteen mazes were being made. But it also meant that we as adults were responsible for the safety of pupils who were not normally part of our class.

Mr Canning said that, in his experience, as pupils varied in the length of time they took to make their mazes, we only needed four glue guns. These will all be placed on top of the low cupboards at the side of the classroom so they can be plugged into sockets without their leads trailing on the floor. Pupils will bring their mazes to the glue guns as and when they are needed. My role will be to supervise the use of these glue guns. This means that I need to ensure the safety of all the pupils using the guns and to ensure my own safety – it is just as easy for me to get burnt as the children.

We discussed whether the pupils needed to wear safety goggles as they sawed the wood, the activity which Mr Canning would be supervising, and agreed that for this activity they would not need them as balsa wood did not send out splinters.

Keeping the learning environment safe and as free from hazards as possible during the activity

My specific area of responsibility for this lesson was the row of low cupboards along one wall of the classroom. There are two double sockets in the wall just above the cupboards into which the four glue guns were to be plugged. The lesson took place in an afternoon. During the preceding lunchtime I cleared the top of the cupboards of everything else – placing the files and boxes which are normally kept there inside the cupboards. In this way I made sure that the only things out in that part of the learning environment were the glue guns. I placed spare tubes of glue in a tray at one end of the cupboard surface. I also covered the surface of the cupboards with a long cloth so that any glue spilled would go onto that. During the activity I made sure that this cloth remained flat.

Neither Mr Canning nor I wanted children queuing up at the cupboards waiting to use the glue guns as this would have created a risk. When explaining the activity to the class, therefore, Mr Canning had told the pupils that only four pairs of pupils at a time were allowed to come to the glue gun area. He explained carefully how to use the guns and pointed out the dangers. The ends of the guns themselves get hot and the glue itself, as it is extruded in liquid form, is also hot, even though it cools down quite quickly.

During the activity I made sure that only the required number of pupils used the guns, I sent others back to their seats to wait their turn.

Using equipment correctly and safely

I watched over the Year 4 pupils as they used the glue guns, making sure they were using them properly. I made sure that no one messed about and they all followed the procedures they had been shown.

Storing equipment safely

After the activity I waited until the glue guns had cooled down and returned them to their boxes and returned them to the top shelf of the cupboard in the resources room which is used only by teachers. I stored unused sticks of glue in their boxes and placed them alongside the guns. I also helped Mr Canning put away the saws and unused pieces of wood and ball bearings in the same cupboard.

Disposing of waste and spillage

After all the equipment had been put away I gathered up the cloth, which had a fair amount of glue stuck to it, and disposed of this in the big bins in the school playground.

I watched over a few pupils as they were asked to collect up all the bits of wood and plastic that were left over as waste – both from the tables and from the floor. I made sure that everything was placed in a large black bin liner, which I took to the bins along with the cloth.

Teacher's comments

Miranda is very knowledgeable about aspects of health and safety and worked within the school's guidelines in this situation.

I certify that this is a true statement of what occurred.

Teacher's signature	Name (printed and role)
J Canning	Jacob Canning, Class Teacher

Assessor's comments

Miranda, again your personal account is clearly structured into sections which refer to the performance indicators you should be covering. I am sure this helped you to write such an account. In this personal account you demonstrate knowledge regarding health and safety matters. We will follow this up in class next time we meet. I will ask you questions relating to health and safety matters. I will record your answers and then we will be able to sign off some of your knowledge base indicators. Remember to include the risk assessment form as this is good evidence.

Signed: Terrie Cole

Terrie Cole
NVQ Assessor

Personal Account
Name: Miranda Appleton
Date: 24 April 2006
3.10.1 Contribute to the maintenance of a safe and secure learning environment

Y2 Science investigation and fire drill

Information regarding my own whereabouts

I had agreed with Miss Grey, the class teacher, to take a group of six Year 2 pupils into the far playground to conduct the science investigation for two reasons. One, because that was where the outside tap was from which the plastic tank could be filled with water. Two, to practise a fire drill when I am working with a group of pupils outside of the class.

Although Miss Grey knew where I was, I also told the office staff where I would be. The two school secretaries have the responsibility for sweeping the school in the event of a fire to make sure that all adults and pupils have evacuated the building in response to an alarm. They therefore need to know where everybody is at any one time.

Implement appropriate safety procedures without delay in an emergency

When the fire alarm went off I put into action what Miss Grey and I had agreed. My priority was to get the children out of the building by the quickest route. We did not, therefore, go to join the rest of class as this would have taken us back into the building. Instead, I lined the six pupils up in pairs and walked with them out of the playground and out of the school gate, joining in with another class who was going through the gate at the same time. All the school lined up just along the street in front of the local church in their classes. I took the six pupils, walked with them along the street and lined up in the place where Miss Grey's class would be. The rest of the class joined us a couple of minutes later and Miss Grey took the register to make sure that all the children present in school that day were lined up, which they were.

Teacher's comments

Miranda and I discussed all aspects of the fire drill and I was very pleased to see that she followed the guidelines.

I certify that this is a true statement of what occurred.

Teacher's signature	Name (printed and role)
E Grey	Emily Grey, Class Teacher

Assessor's comments

Again, well done.

Signed: Terrie Cole

Terrie Cole
NVQ Assessor

3.10.2 Minimise the risks arising from health emergencies

Setting the scene

Miranda is on duty in the Key Stage 1 playground during morning break. There are three playgrounds and class teachers are on duty in the other two. None of the playgrounds is visible to each other. Miranda is informed that a pupil has fallen over and appears to be seriously hurt, she is crying, her ankle is twisted under her and she is unable to get up from the ground. A large group of children are beginning to gather around her.

Writing personal accounts: covering performance indicators

When writing up what she has seen and done, Miranda needs to make reference to the following performance indicators.

Unit 3.10.2 Minimise the risks arising from health emergencies

Performance indicators	*Scope of emergencies*
(1) Immediately summon assistance for any health *emergencies* and begin action appropriate to the condition. (2) Provide the individual with the health *emergency* with support, both verbally and by physical presence. (3) Give appropriate support to assist in the ongoing care of the individual with the health *emergency* when someone with more competence to deal with the emergency is available. (4) Do what you can to make the immediate vicinity as private and safe as possible once the appropriate person has taken over responsibility for dealing with the individual with the health *emergency*. (5) Offer appropriate support to any others involved in the incident once the initial danger has passed. (6) Comply with legal and school requirements for recording accidents and *emergencies*.	(a) Severe bleeding (b) Cardiac arrest (c) Shock (d) Faints or loss of consciousness (e) Epileptic seizure (f) Choking and difficulty with breathing (g) Falls – potential and actual fractures (h) Burns and scalds (i) Poisoning (j) Electrocution (k) Substance abuse

Personal Account

Name: Miranda Appleton
Date: 28 April 2006
3.10.2 Minimise the risks arising from health emergencies

Immediately summon assistance for any health emergencies and begin action appropriate to the condition

When I went over to Pamela I saw that she was very distressed, crying and in a lot of pain. Her leg was in an awkward position under her body and she was complaining that her ankle hurt. I had been told to treat any possible fracture as an actual fracture, so took this very seriously.

As I was not trained in first aid, I did not touch her myself but sent two pupils I knew to be sensible to run to the school office to ask the school administration officer and the head teacher to come as quickly as possible.

Provide the individual with the health emergency with support, both verbally and by physical presence

After the pupils had gone I continued speaking with Pamela, reassuring her that help was on its way. I took off my jacket and puffed it up, placing it under Pamela's head like a pillow to make her more comfortable. I held her hand to give her comfort and gently wiped her forehead with my other hand.

Give appropriate support to assist in the ongoing care of the individual with the health emergency when someone with more competence to deal with the emergency is available

Within two minutes the administration officer (trained in first aid) and the head teacher both arrived. They, too, agreed that Pamela could have potentially fractured her ankle and that she should not be moved. I was asked to go to the office as quickly as possible to ask the school secretary to summon an ambulance and contact Pamela's parents. This I did.

Do what you can to make the immediate vicinity as private and safe as possible once the appropriate person has taken over responsibility for dealing with the individual with the health emergency

While we were waiting for the other members of staff to come, I asked the other pupils to move right away from Pamela. Two of her close friends stayed with her, but the others spread out around the playground. Some began playing again, but most stood still watching from a distance. The playground was unusually quiet, but this benefited Pamela, who was not distressed by shouting and movement around her.

Having asked for the ambulance to be called, I returned to the playground and, at the request of the head teacher, dismissed all the pupils back to their classes. I then went to the staff room to inform the teachers what had happened. Pamela's class teacher immediately came out to see her, so I went in to cover her class until she got back.

Offer appropriate support to any others involved in the incident once the initial danger has passed

The ambulance came within fifteen minutes, and by then Pamela's mother had arrived as well. The ambulance crew agreed that Pamela had probably suffered a fracture and took her to hospital.

Back in school a good number of pupils, particularly Pamela's friends, were distressed. Along with other teachers and TAs I spent time with some of them in the class letting them cry, putting my arms around them and reassuring them that she would be all right, that she was in the best place and getting the attention she needed.

It was distressing for us all, but I hope I maintained a calm exterior throughout giving confidence to pupils around me. Once it was all over I needed to go into the staff room and sit by myself for a bit with a cup of strong tea.

Comply with legal and school requirements for recording accidents and emergencies

I complied with legal and school requirements in this incident by responding immediately and by not going beyond my own training and qualifications.

After the incident had been dealt with I went to the school office and wrote my account in the school accident log. The school secretary had already noted the incident and logged the time of calling the ambulance and the parents.

Teacher's comments

This was clearly a difficult situation which Miranda handled well.

I certify that this is a true statement of what occurred.

Staff signature	Name (printed and role)
M Biggins	Mabel Biggins, School Administration Officer

Assessor's comments

I agree with the Administration Officer's comments. Well done. Can you let me have a copy of the accident log as further evidence? Again, remember confidentiality and block out names.

Signed: Terrie Cole

Terrie Cole
NVQ Assessor

Chapter 10

Unit 3.11 Contribute to the health and well-being of pupils

In this unit there are three elements:

3.11.1 Support pupils in adjusting to a new setting
3.11.2 Support pupils in maintaining standards of health and hygiene
3.11.3 Respond to signs of health problems

KNOWLEDGE BASE

3.11.1 Support pupils in adjusting to a new setting

In order to most effectively support pupils settle into new situations, you need to know quite a lot, but you also need to use your common sense.

Different strategies to use for helping pupils adjust to a new setting

Most children adjust readily to new settings, but there are particular times when more support may be needed. The most obvious is starting at a new school – either in Reception or at times of transition. However, an individual pupil joining an existing class part way through a year or a pupil rejoining a class after prolonged absence, perhaps through illness, may need support as well.

Strategies to help pupils settle in are likely to include:

- being shown around the school
- being introduced to members of staff
- being introduced to other children
- being made to feel welcome and part of the class (in primary school it helps to have places and trays labelled)
- jointly agreeing class rules and routines so that each pupil feels an 'ownership' of the class.

Above all else, being friendly and available as a TA to pupils is a vital part of helping pupils settle in.

School policies and procedures for helping pupils adjust to a new setting

Your school will have agreed strategies to help pupils settle in. Some strategies may in fact be recommended by the local authority. This may especially be true for pupils returning after long periods of illness, for pupils who are being reintegrated back into school after a permanent exclusion from another school, or for pupils who have little or no spoken English. This is particularly the case for refugees or asylum seekers. If you are asked to support such pupils you need to make sure you are familiar with your school's policies and procedures for these pupils as they will each present with particular needs (see Figure 10.1).

The sort of factors e.g. age, care history, home background, EAL, special educational needs, that might affect a pupil's ability to adjust to a new setting and what additional support may be needed

Pupils who are self-confident and arrive at a new setting with a positive experience of school may not need much support in helping to settle in. However, not all pupils come to a new class like this. Many factors may make it harder for the pupil to settle in:

- The home background may have been disturbed or even traumatic.
- Children Looked After may find it hard to settle due to the levels of change, loss and uncertainty which they have experienced.
- Those from other cultures and speaking another language may find the whole initial experience of school alien and frightening. Some may never have been to school

Figure 10.1 TAs can help pupils settle into the school environment

before or, if they have, their experience of school can have been very different from a school in Britain.
- Pupils with special educational needs may find it harder to settle than others for a variety of reasons – some may not fully understand what is happening around them while for others part of their need itself is difficulty responding to change.

All these pupils may need time being spent with them by a sympathetic and understanding TA to help them overcome their particular barriers to settling in. Any such support will need to be agreed following discussions between teachers, parents or carers, TAs and the SENCO.

The sorts of problems with adjusting to a new setting that might occur, and how to recognise and respond to these

Two extreme responses to problems settling in might be called ‘fight or flight’. At the one extreme, pupils might refuse to come into school, shout and scream at the school entrance, cling to the gates and so on. At the other extreme, pupils may withdraw into themselves and sit, almost cowering in the class, saying nothing and doing nothing and refusing to be drawn out. In secondary schools students may simply choose to ‘bunk off’.

Such behaviours present challenges to the adults working with these pupils. There is no easy or obvious answer. Time and effort are required to get alongside the pupils, seek to calm their fears and build an assurance that things will be alright. If these types of behaviour persist, expert help may need to be called upon via the school’s SENCO.

The likelihood is, however, that any problems adjusting to new settings experienced by pupils you support will be somewhere between these extremes. In this case, the problem can be harder to spot. It is important to be on the lookout for all new pupils to spot any significant change in behaviour or attitude, any obvious signs of distress such as crying or any uncharacteristic responses to work or to others in the class. Any or all of these can indicate that something is troubling the pupil, preventing them from feeling settled and secure.

Whatever the specific sign of distress, the most important response you can give is time and attention. Giving the pupil opportunity to talk, to show they are valued and important is crucial in helping them overcome their insecurities. Asking open ended questions in a non-confrontational way may help them identify any specific area of concern which you can then help overcome.

Checklist

- ✔ I am familiar with my school’s strategies for helping pupils adjust to a new setting.
- ✔ I am aware of the factors which may make it difficult for a pupil to adjust to a new setting.
- ✔ I know how to respond to pupils who are finding it difficult to settle in.

3.11.2 Support pupils in maintaining standards of health and hygiene

(See also Unit 3.10 Support the maintenance of pupil safety and security.)

Class routines relating to meeting physical needs

Teachers will have their own routines and procedures relating to the physical needs of the pupils. You and the class teacher need to agree the areas where you can take the initiative and where you need to leave things to the teacher.

Methods of caring for personal hygiene and the variations in family or cultural backgrounds and settings

Pupils may vary in their views on personal hygiene depending on their family or cultural backgrounds. You need to be aware of this and respond accordingly. For instance, there may be an outbreak of head lice in your school; one pupil is deeply ashamed of having them whereas another does not seem to be bothered. Both present challenges to which you need to respond.

How pupil's age, gender, cultural or racial background and specific medical conditions affect their personal hygiene requirements

Clearly, the younger the child the more they are likely to need support with personal hygiene. The youngest pupils will need to have basic hygiene routines taught and reinforced whereas these, we hope, would be well established in older pupils. However, some older pupils may still need to have these routines emphasised. A pupil, for instance, on the autistic spectrum may need to be constantly reminded to wash his hands after using the toilet or, alternatively, taught that he does not need to wash his hands every half hour or so. Pupils from certain cultures may also be more sensitive to the need of a high level of personal hygiene and cleanliness than others. You need to be aware of the make-up of your class and respond accordingly.

Sources of medical and health care, how these can be accessed, and who is qualified to deal with different needs

Within school there will be members of staff responsible for health and safety, child protection and the distribution of medication. You need to be aware of who these people are and find out your school procedures to access them. Your first port of call is going to be the class teacher with whom you work. All schools have access to school nurses and paediatricians. If you have concerns over particular pupils which you think warrant contact with these agencies, you need to inform your class teacher.

When parents or carers would need to be advised of health or hygiene problems and the school policy and procedures for doing this

Your school will have a policy regarding contacting parents in the event of health or hygiene issues. You need to become familiar with this. In many cases parents will be contacted via school office staff rather than by individual teachers or TAs.

School policy for health education

Health education is part of the National Curriculum and is normally covered within PSHE (personal, social and hygiene education). Exactly what is covered and how this subject is taught will differ depending on the age of the pupils in the school, but the overall aim will be to develop a sense of personal responsibility and pride in pupils and give them information to make informed choices about their lifestyles. This will be in keeping with the *Every Child Matters* outcome: Be Healthy.

School policies with regard to health, hygiene and medical issues

The school's Health and Safety Policy should include matters relating to hygiene and medical issues. Every school will have a method of recording pupils' medical details, usually as part of the registration form completed by parents or carers which is regularly updated. These details will include the name, address and telephone number of the family's general practitioner (GP), whether or not the child has any allergies and information regarding any medication the pupil needs to take.

School policy for medicines in school and how this relates to national and local policies

Every school's Health and Safety Policy should address similar issues – the type of medicines allowed in school, the measures taken to ensure their appropriate use and their safe-keeping, the members of staff available to administer medicines and so on. All this has to relate to local authority and to government policies and procedures.

Legal and organisational requirements relating to child protection issues and their implications for attending to pupils' hygiene, health and medical needs and for reporting concerns about pupils' health and well-being

It may be that the first signs of issues relating to child protection are seen in their personal hygiene. Perhaps a child is continually dirty with clothes never changed and hair not washed over an extended period of time. This could be evidence of neglect. You have a legal duty to report your concerns to the class teacher or directly to the school's Child Protection Liaison Officer.

How to maintain your own health and safety when attending to pupils' hygiene, health and medical needs

At all times you should have concern for your own health and safety so, for instance, you need to wear protective clothing such as latex gloves, when touching or potentially touching any bodily fluid. If a child is physically sick, you must not clear it up yourself – instead the caretaker needs to be informed so that he or she can deal with it.

No member of staff is obliged to administer medicines but, if they volunteer to do so, they must be fully trained and rehearsed. If you have not received such training, do not administer any medication.

Checklist

- ✔ After talking with the teacher(s) I work with, I know the areas where I can use my initiative in supporting pupils make healthy and hygienic choices and where I need to refer to the teacher(s).
- ✔ I am familiar with my school's procedures for accessing support regarding health and hygiene matters.
- ✔ I am familiar with my school's policy and procedures regarding health education.
- ✔ I am familiar with my school's policy and procedures regarding medication in school.

3.11.3 Respond to signs of health problems

Signs and symptoms of common illnesses and sources of help in identification and response

Refer to the table on page 164.

Factors such as medical conditions, religion, culture, to be taken into account when responding to signs of ill-health

If signs of health problems begin to show, a pupil with a recognised medical condition is likely to need more careful supervision than an otherwise healthy child (see Figure 10.2). It is important to be aware of children in your class who have a medical condition as that could complicate an otherwise reasonably straightforward situation. A pupil with asthma, say, may well react severely to the onset of a cold.

Illness and symptoms	*Response*
Colds and flu – runny nose, coughing, temperature, difficulty breathing	Rest at home; infectious; medicines available from a pharmacy; see GP if symptoms persist
Chickenpox – itchy red spots with white centres on parts of the body	Infectious; keep at home for five days after the rash begins; calamine lotion to ease itching; can be very serious in adults
German measles (rubella) – pink rash on head, torso, arms and legs, slight fever, sore throat	Infectious particularly before diagnosis is possible; keep indoors for five days from onset of rash; keep away from pregnant women
Impetigo – small red pimples on skin which weep	Infectious – stay at home until all weeping has stopped; treat with antibiotics from GP
Ringworm – infection of the skin, flaky circles under the skin	Contagious; see GP for antibiotics
Diarrhoea and sickness	Keep taking fluids; keep at home until 24 hours after sickness and diarrhoea has stopped; see GP if persists
Conjunctivitis – redness and sore eyelids and around the eyes, irritant	Infectious; swab with warm water; visit GP if persists; school may have a policy on length of time to stay at home
Measles – fever, runny eyes, sore throat and cough, red rash over the body	Rest; lots of fluid; visit GP if symptoms persist; some form of junior painkiller to reduce fever
Tonsillitis – very sore throat, tonsils enlarged, fever, earache	See GP and treat with antibiotics; frequent and/or severe cases may require surgery
Meningitis – severe headache, fever, stiff neck, rash on skin which does not go when pressed with a glass	See GP immediately or call ambulance urgently – can be fatal

Figure 10.2 'Miss, I don't feel well!'

School policy and procedures for recording and reporting incidents, significant medical conditions, administration of medicines and communicable diseases, and your role and responsibilities in relation to this

The school's Health and Safety Policy will detail procedures for responding to health problems. You need to be familiar with this so you follow the appropriate procedure. It is vital that the correct person or persons be informed at the earliest opportunity if any such health problem arises.

If cases of head lice or ringworm or other conditions which are contagious occur in your school, there will be a procedure for informing parents. Normally this will be in the form of a letter going home or it may be as an insert in a regular newsletter. Either way, parents will need to be informed that there is a contagious condition within the school and will be given advice as to how best to respond to it.

Your role is to reinforce the school policy and procedures. It is important not to go beyond them.

Checklist

- ✔ I can recognise the symptoms of common childhood illnesses and health problems.
- ✔ I know how to respond to such health problems.
- ✔ I am familiar with my school's policy and procedures for reporting and recording health problems.

MEETING PERFORMANCE INDICATORS

3.11.1 Support pupils in adjusting to a new setting

Setting the scene

Nazreen is working in a Year 3 class of thirty in a junior school. It is the first day of the new academic year. The pupils have come from a mixture of three feeder infant schools.

Writing personal accounts: covering performance indicators

When writing up what she has seen and done, Nazreen makes reference to the following performance indicators.

Unit 3.11.1 Support pupils in adjusting to a new setting

Performance indicators	*Scope of information*
(1) Contribute to strategies designed to help pupils join in activities and adjust to the *setting*. (2) Offer reassurance and *information* as required by the pupil to help him/her learn about the new *setting*. (3) Positively encourage other pupils to interact with and welcome new arrivals (4) Promptly recognise signs of distress and respond appropriately as agreed with the teacher (5) Promptly report any problems in helping pupils adjust to the *setting* to the teacher	Scope of *settings* (a) New pupil(s) joining the class (b) Transition into a new class at the start of the year (c) Pupils rejoining a class after extended absence Scope of *information* (a) School and class policies and rules (b) Layout of school/class and the locations of different areas and equipment (c) Staff and other pupils with whom the pupil will interact (d) Class routines

Personal Account

Name: Nazreen Begum
Date: 4 September 2006
3.11.1 Support pupils in adjusting to a new setting – new Year 3 class

---

Contribute to strategies designed to help pupils join in activities and adjust to the setting

Mrs Russell and I had met up at the end of the previous term to plan how we were going to help the new class settle in. We had met the class twice during the last term and had begun to learn their names. Through discussion with their previous teachers and reading their records from the infant schools we had begun to build up a picture of them.

Our agreed aim for the first day was to make each pupil feel secure and settled in the class. All but two of the pupils were coming from feeder schools with pupils they already knew. Two pupils were new to the area and therefore did not know anybody.

We had agreed on the following strategies:

Name tags and labels

On the last day of the previous term I had typed out the names of all the pupils in the new class on strips of card which Mrs Russell had placed onto each pupil's personal tray. I had also printed name tags which Mrs Russell stuck next to coat hooks just outside the class. In this way we hoped that each pupil would feel they belonged to the class and already had a place in it.

Seating plan

During the previous term, Mrs Russell and I had worked out the groups we wanted the children to sit in. We sought to mix up children from the different schools, while ensuring that each pupil had at least one person they knew to sit next to. We placed the two children from out of the area next to pupils we knew to be friendly and caring. In this way we wanted to give each child a sense of continuity with the past, yet expand them to embrace the new of the current situation.

Activities

Mrs Russell and I had planned the first day's activities to be fun, not to be too taxing, but nevertheless to set a standard that hard work would be expected from everyone. During the first lesson each child was to produce a self-portrait in coloured pencils which would go on to a class display. Under each portrait the pupils would write their names, one thing about their families and one thing they were looking forward to in their new school.

Photographs

During the course of the morning, as agreed with Mrs Russell, I took digital photographs of each of the pupils and printed these out over lunchtime. This meant that, by the afternoon, we were ready to pin photographs up next to the self-portraits. In this way we sought to reinforce the sense of belonging and being welcomed into the new class.

Offer reassurance and information as required by the pupil to help him/her learn about the new setting

All the pupils were new to the setting and so, at the beginning of the day, they all needed to know the same information. As agreed with Mrs Russell, once the initial welcome was made to the class as a whole, places allocated and the classroom routine laid out, I took the pupils out in their groups (either of six or eight). I took them on a tour of the school to show them where everything was. Those remaining in class continued working on their self-portraits with Mrs Russell.

I showed them the boys' and girls' toilets, the hall, the other classrooms, the school office, the head teacher's office, the ICT suite, the staff room and the music room. I showed them the exits into the playgrounds and where the water fountains were.

As we went round I answered any questions they had about the school and what went on here.

Positively encourage other pupils to interact with and welcome new arrivals

I was especially conscious of the two pupils from out of the area – both girls. I made a special point of meeting them and welcoming them in the playground as the class began to line up. In so doing I also met their mothers, who were equally anxious. I walked with the two girls into the school, asking them about their previous schools and explaining to them the procedures for coming into this school.

Once in the class I introduced each of them to the pupils they were to sit next to and kept an eye on them throughout the day. As the pupils we had chosen them to sit with were friendly and welcoming I knew it would not be too much of an issue. The next day I was very pleased to receive a 'thank you note' from one of the parents thanking me for my support.

Promptly recognise signs of distress and respond appropriately as agreed with the teacher

Most children were very happy during the day, but towards lunchtime I noticed that one boy had become quite tearful. He sat in his place, not making a fuss, but he had stopped his activity and was looking down at the table. As I went over to him, I saw that he was wiping his eyes, trying not to cry.

This was not an uncommon experience and I had agreed with Mrs Russell that, if appropriate, I should take any pupil in distress to one side and talk quietly with them. I knelt down beside the boy to speak at his level and spoke gently, 'Is everything all right?' 'I miss my mum,' he replied and began to really cry. I asked him if he would like to take a little walk and he said he would. So he and I went and sat just outside of the classroom in a shared work area. I asked him about home and what he had done over the summer holidays. We chatted about holidays and about school and after a few minutes he cheered up. I reassured him that his mum would be there in a couple of hours at the end of the school day. We went back into class and after that he was fine.

Promptly report any problems in helping pupils adjust to the setting to the teacher

The only real problem I came across during that first day was one of the pupils with English as an additional language had not understood very much of what had been told her during the day. As soon as I became aware of this I told Mrs Russell and she agreed that she would need to contact the local authority's support service to try to get someone who spoke this pupil's first language to explain things to her.

Teacher's comments

Nazreen was of great assistance during what can be for some pupils a difficult day. I appreciate her comments about those pupils experiencing particular difficulties.

I certify that this is a true statement of what occurred.

Teacher's signature	Name (printed and role)
K Russell	Katie Russell, Class Teacher

Assessor's comments

A clearly structured personal account using the performance indicators to provide a framework for your account. You clearly have the knowledge and skills to meet the performance indicators and much of this account can be used as evidence to show this. However, when you took the group around the school there was no one to specifically witness you doing this. Offering reassurance as required to help pupils learn about a new setting is something you will be doing frequently over the next few weeks. You could write another account, possibly in the form of a diary which could be witnessed by the teacher, or perhaps the teacher could write a brief witness statement giving an example of how you do this.

As part of your evidence, could you let me have a copy of the letter sent to you by the parent? You will need to blot out any names to respect confidentiality.

Signed: Terrie Cole

Terrie Cole
NVQ Assessor

3.11.2 Support pupils in maintaining standards of health and hygiene

Setting the scene

During their first week in school concerns arise over one pupil in Mrs Russell's class. Eric's infant school reported that, on occasion, he had soiled himself. He does not seem to recognise when he wants to use the toilet, and, by the time he does so, it is sometimes too late. Nazreen has been asked by Mrs Russell to specifically talk with Eric about this and show him the routines for using the toilets.

Writing personal accounts: covering performance indicators

When writing up what she has seen and done, Nazreen makes reference to the following performance indicators.

Unit 3.11.2 Support pupils in maintaining standards of health and hygiene

Performance indicators	*Scope*
(1) Provide advice and assistance as required to enable pupils to develop basic hygiene skills. (2) Support pupils in respecting their own and others' needs relating to health and hygiene matters. (3) Assist pupils to access appropriate *medical and health care* when needed. (4) Follow school policy in responding to questions about health and medical matters from a pupil. (5) Follow health and safety regulations and guidelines when attending to pupils' hygiene, health and medical needs. (6) Promptly report any problems in maintaining standards of health and hygiene to the teacher.	Scope of *medical and health care* (a) Health and hygiene specific to an individual pupil's condition (b) Basic health and hygiene (c) Access to first aid (d) Health care matters affecting the whole class or school

Personal Account

Name: Nazreen Begum
Date: 8 September 2006
3.11.2 Support pupils in maintaining standards of health and hygiene

Provide advice and assistance as required to enable pupils to develop basic hygiene skills

This morning it became apparent that Eric had soiled himself. There was a nasty smell around him and he was obviously in some discomfort. I had already made a point of getting to know Eric over the previous two days and I felt he was comfortable with me. I followed what had been agreed with Mrs Russell if such an event occurred.

I went over to him and quietly asked him if he was all right. He shook his head. I asked him if he would come to the side of the class with me, which he did. I said, 'I think you've been to the toilet.' And Eric again nodded his head. I assured him that it was OK and that he would not get into any trouble for it, but said that he would need to get cleaned up and put on another pair of trousers.

He went to the toilet to clean himself up and to put on his PE shorts. In the mean time I went to the school office to ask them to phone his mum. She came in within fifteen minutes to help clean him up properly and to provide him with a new pair of pants and trousers.

While we were waiting for his mum, Eric and I sat in a quiet area outside the class. I put on latex gloves and placed his soiled clothes inside a carrier bag, tying the ends up. I then disposed of the gloves in the appropriate container in the school office and washed my hands. I made sure he had washed his hands after cleaning himself up and we talked about using the toilet in time. It seems he is embarrassed to ask to go and will try and 'hang on' until playtime. Sometimes this works, but this morning it didn't. I agreed with Eric that, if ever he felt he needed to go to the toilet he did not have to put his hand up in front of the whole class, he could signal to me and I would come over and give him permission to go. I checked this out later with Mrs Russell and she was very happy about this.

Support pupils in respecting their own and others' needs relating to health and hygiene matters

When talking with Eric I stressed how important it was for him to feel comfortable about going to the toilet – that it was natural, everybody did it and there is nothing to be ashamed of. I also said that other children would rather he asked to go to the toilet than 'make a mistake' during the lesson. He understood all this and said he would try to respond more quickly to his needs. He already knew how to use the toilet properly and about washing his hands afterwards, but I emphasised this with him as well. Mrs Russell had a word with him later about this as well.

Assist pupils to access appropriate medical and health care when needed

While this may not be a medical condition, there is some concern that it could develop into one. I met with Eric's mum when she brought the trousers in and we talked about visiting the doctor. She said that he had attended a bed-wetting clinic when he was younger. She agreed to take him to the doctors if the problem persisted. She also agreed to leave a spare pair of pants and trousers in the school office in case of future 'accidents'.

Follow school policy in responding to questions about health and medical matters from a pupil

In dealing with this event I followed school policy by putting the pupil at ease as far as possible, by not making him feel embarrassed or 'odd' and by reacting calmly in a measured way. I did not draw attention to his situation but spoke with him as privately as the situation allowed.

Follow health and safety regulations and guidelines when attending to pupils' hygiene, health and medical needs

I followed regulations in this situation by asking Eric to clean himself up rather than going into the toilet with him to help him. If he had not been able to help himself, I would have asked one of the office staff to come with me to help him. I am aware that I should not go into the toilet with him on my own.

I also followed guidelines by asking the office staff to contact Eric's mother as soon as possible, by wearing gloves when possibly coming into contact with bodily fluids and by disposing of the gloves appropriately.

Promptly report any problems in maintaining standards of health and hygiene to the teacher

Once Eric's mum had been and he had a new pair of pants and trousers on (i.e. after about half an hour) he was happy to go back into the class. I went with him and spoke briefly to Mrs Russell saying that everything was now OK. During break I gave her more detailed information about what had taken place. We agreed that we needed to monitor Eric closely and that Mrs Russell would contact his mum immediately if there was any reoccurrence so she could seek medical advice.

Teacher's comments

I took the opportunity later in the day to discuss with Eric what had happened. He was very relieved that Nazreen had, as he said, got him out of a 'sticky situation' and that she had made him feel OK about what had happened. He told me that, if he had to go to the toilet quickly again, he knew he could rely on Nazreen. Eric's mother also thanked me for dealing with the situation and she said that Nazreen had been very helpful. Overall, a very delicate situation sensitively handled.

I certify that this is a true statement of what occurred.

Teacher's signature	Name (printed and role)
K Russell	Katie Russell, Class Teacher

Assessor's comments

Indeed, a very delicate situation that was sensitively handled – well done. Your teacher's comments were needed to authenticate this piece of evidence as much of what occurred was in private and therefore could not be witnessed. Does your school have an Intimate Care Policy? If it does it might be useful to summarise this briefly and include it in your portfolio.

Signed: Terrie Cole

Terrie Cole
NVQ Assessor

3.11.3 Respond to signs of health problems

Setting the scene

Led by their teacher, Nazreen's Year 3 class goes on a trip to a local museum. Nazreen and three mothers accompany them. Each of the five adults has a group of six pupils to look after. One of the pupils in Nazreen's group has medication for asthma in school and can develop symptoms after walking for only a short period of time.

Writing personal accounts: covering performance indicators

When writing up what she has seen and done, Nazreen makes reference to the following performance indicators.

Unit 3.11.3 Respond to signs of health problems

Performance indicators	*Scope of particular health needs*
(1) Recognise and respond promptly to changes in behaviour and well-being which are signs of common illnesses in children and young people.	(a) Asthma (b) Diabetes (c) Incontinence (d) Allergies
(2) Recognise and respond promptly to signs of health problems in a pupil with *particular health needs*.	
(3) Promptly report signs of health problems to the teacher.	
(4) Immediately summon assistance for any health emergency and take action appropriate to the condition, circumstances and boundaries of your role.	
(5) Give reassurance, support, information and advice to the pupil in a manner and place which is appropriate to their age, stage of development and circumstances.	
(6) Recognise the signs of mental or emotional distress and respond in a manner consistent with your role, and school polices and procedures.	
(7) Comply with school policy and procedures for recording information about pupils' health, including issues of confidentiality.	

Note: In the context of NVQ/SVQ assessments, simulations may be used to obtain evidence in relation to responding to health emergencies.

Personal Account

Name: Nazreen Begum
Date: 15 June 2006
3.11.3 Respond to signs of health problems

Recognise and respond promptly to changes in behaviour and well-being which are signs of common illnesses in children and young people

[Nazreen will need to refer to another case study to meet this performance indicator.]

Recognise and respond promptly to signs of health problems in a pupil with particular health needs

As the museum is less than a mile from the school we decided to walk the class to it. Prior to going on the trip Mrs Russell and I had undertaken a risk assessment on each child in the class. We noted that Abigail suffers from asthma. After speaking with Abigail and her mother we agreed that Abigail should come on the trip. She would probably be all right on the walk. The actual visit round the museum should not be a problem at all.

Abigail was in my group on the way to the museum and I carried her inhaler. We were nearly there when I noticed that she had begun to find it difficult to breathe and was beginning to wheeze. She stopped walking and begun to inhale and exhale deeply and was obviously beginning to be distressed.

Abigail herself was used to what was happening, and I was prepared for it. I asked the whole group to stop and gave Abigail her inhaler. I made sure the other pupils gave her space as she used her inhaler. It took a couple of minutes to take effect, during which time the whole class was waiting on the pavement away from the kerb. After that she recovered and was able to reach the museum. At the museum I made sure she sat down and rested for ten minutes before engaging with the rest of the visit. There were no more incidents during the day.

Promptly report signs of health problems to the teacher

As soon as I realised Abigail was having an asthma attack I sent a pupil to go ahead to the front of the class to tell Mrs Russell. She stopped the class on the pavement as soon as she heard and came back to see how Abigail was.

Immediately summon assistance for any health emergency and take action appropriate to the condition, circumstances and boundaries of your role

My role was to be on hand to give the medication to Abigail. She herself was experienced in the using of it, but I supervised her in any case. In this instance there was no need to call the emergency services or any other assistance as she made a full recovery.

Give reassurance, support, information and advice to the pupil in a manner and place which is appropriate to their age, stage of development and circumstances

Throughout the episode I stayed next to Abigail, giving her verbal reassurance that everything would be all right and that the class would wait with her. During the attack Abigail tried to speak to say she was sorry for holding everybody up. I assured her that she did not need to worry and suggested to her that she should not try to talk.

Recognise the signs of mental or emotional distress and respond in a manner consistent with your role, and school polices and procedures

In line with school policy, I had the appropriate medication to hand and gave it immediately, supervising its use. I also made sure that Abigail had space around her and did not feel hemmed in by other pupils.

Comply with school policy and procedures for recording information about pupils' health, including issues of confidentiality

As soon as the incident was over, I used my mobile phone to contact the school office to say what had happened. We did not feel it was necessary to contact Abigail's mother as she seemed to have recovered fully. This was in line with what we had agreed with Abigail and her mother before the visit.

When we arrived back at school I wrote down an account of the incident in the school accident book, in accordance with school policy. This was countersigned by Mrs Russell. Mrs Russell wrote a note for Abigail's mother for her to take home with her.

Teacher's comments

Nazreen followed the current procedures as outlined in the school's Health and Safety Policy. It was easy to see that Abigail felt much more at ease about what was happening due to Nazreen's assistance.

I certify that this is a true statement of what occurred.

Teacher's signature	Name (printed and role)
K Russell	Katie Russell, Class Teacher

Assessor's comments

Another difficult situation sensitively and effectively handled. You are a real asset to your school. Remember to include a copy of the risk assessment form and a photocopy of the log of the incident as evidence.

Signed: Terrie Cole

Terrie Cole
NVQ Assessor

Memo to Terrie Cole from Nazreen Begum (NVQ 2 student)

As requested – please find enclosed a copy of the risk assessment form and accident log referred to in my personal account. Although we conducted a risk assessment on a number of individual pupils, I have only included the information relating to Abigail.

Somewhere Junior School Risk Assessment and Risk Management Form – educational visits

Location of the visit: City Museum | Purpose of visit: Local history study
Group on the visit: Class 3R | Leader: Mrs Russell (class teacher)
Other accompanying adults: Miss Begum (TA) and three mothers
Group size: 30 | Adult-pupil ratio: 1:6

Identifying and assessing risks	*What to do to reduce the risk*
Location of visit	
Walk along a main road, crossing several smaller ones	Split into groups of six, each leader practised in 'shepherding' pupils across roads
Risk rating high	Reduced risk level low
Complex corridors and rooms out of sight from each other	Group leaders regularly take head count
Risk rating high	Reduced risk level low
Risk to group as a whole	
30 children mixed ability – get separated, misbehave	Low pupil teacher ratio, pupils likely to misbehave with placed with teacher or TA
Risk rating medium	Reduced risk level low
Risk to individual pupils	
Abigail – asthma – can develop symptoms after walking for only a short period of time.	Discussion between TA, teacher and Abigail's mother – agreed TA to have Abigail in her group and take medication and mobile phone with her. Agreed procedures if asthma attack occurs (administer medication and contact school and mother and emergency services if serious)
Risk level medium	Reduced risk level low

Somewhere Junior School Accident/Incident Log

Date of accident/incident: 15.6.06
Time of accident/incident: 9.25 a.m.
Location of accident/incident: Princes Road on way to City Museum
Nature of accident/incident: Asthma attack – Abigail
Name and title of person dealing with the accident/incident:
Nazreen Begum (teaching assistant) under the supervision of Mrs Russell (teacher)
Name and title of person completing this log: Nazreen Begum (TA)
Other person(s) involved including their roles/responsibilities:
Mrs Katie Russell (class teacher)
Any follow up required
None

Description of the accident/incident

Abigail was in my group on the way to the museum. We were nearly there when I noticed that she had begun to find it difficult to breath and was beginning to wheeze. She stopped walking and began to inhale and exhale deeply and was obviously beginning to be distressed.

Response to the accident/incident

Abigail herself was used to what was happening, and I was prepared for it. I asked the whole group to stop and gave Abigail her inhaler. I made sure the other pupils gave her space as she used her inhaler. As soon as I realised Abigail was having an asthma attack I sent a pupil to go ahead to the front of the class to tell Mrs Russell. She stopped the class on the pavement as soon as she heard and came back to see how Abigail was. It took two minutes or so to take effect, during which time the whole class was waiting away from the kerb. After that she recovered and was able to reach the museum. At the museum I made sure she sat down and rested for ten minutes before engaging with the rest of the visit. There were no more incidents during the day.

Signature of person completing this form:
Nazreen Begum (Teaching Assistant)
Date signed: 15.6.06
Reasons for any delay in completing this form:
I completed this form on return to the school after the visit to the museum.

Chapter 11

Unit 3.17 Support the use of ICT in the classroom

In this unit there are two elements:

3.17.1 Prepare ICT equipment for use in the classroom
3.17.2 Support classroom use of ICT equipment

KNOWLEDGE BASE

3.17.1 Prepare ICT equipment for use in the classroom

The sorts of ICT equipment available within school and where it is kept

Although many people tend to think of computers when they hear the term 'ICT', 'information and communication technology' actually refers to any equipment which is designed to carry information electrically or electronically. ICT therefore includes overhead projectors, tape recorders, photographic equipment, DVDs and so on as well as computers, printers, scanners and all peripherals.

One of the exciting features of ICT, and one of its challenges, is the constant technological development taking place. What was 'state of the art' five years ago is now likely to be 'old hat' and need replacing. This means that, if you are going to use ICT, you need to keep up.

Where ICT equipment is stored will vary from school to school. Desktop computers, towers, keyboards, printers and scanners will be housed in classrooms, shared work areas or computer suites. Portable equipment such as laptops, digital cameras and video cameras are likely to be stored securely in lockable cabinets. You need to become familiar with your school procedures, including how to access such secure units and use the equipment stored there.

School procedures for booking or allocating ICT equipment for use in the classroom

The location and use of accessories, consumables and instructions/information texts

Who to report equipment faults and problems to and the procedures for doing this

Many schools employ an ICT technician as well as an ICT manager. One of these is likely to be responsible for organising the distribution of ICT resources, overseeing the location and use of accessories and consumables such as printer ink and paper, and for dealing with problems. Your point of contact, therefore, is likely to be this person.

3.17.2 Support classroom use of ICT equipment

Operating requirements and routines

It is important that all ICT equipment is used as it was designed to be used. Mostly this will be obvious and straightforward, but if you are not sure, read the instruction manual or seek advice. Trying to experiment with ICT equipment can be expensive and even dangerous. It is important that you find out whether you, as a TA, are authorised to unplug computers and/or printers.

Relevant legislation, regulations and guidance in relation to the use of ICT, e.g. copyright, data protection, software licensing, child protection

Schools are covered by national legislation such as the Data Protection Act 1998, the Children Acts 1989 and 2004, and the Freedom of Information Act 2005; for further information see Chapter 13. Copyright legislation and software licensing law will also need to be followed so that all programs are used legally. All members of staff are required to be aware of the implications of legislation when using ICT. Basically it is designed to ensure that information is used appropriately. One aspect of copyright law is that, normally, staff are not allowed to bring software from home and load it on to school equipment.

The school policy for use of ICT in the classroom including virus controls and access to the internet

Each school will have a policy for ICT. You need to be familiar with this policy and follow its guidelines as it will state how and when pupils may access the internet and what they are allowed to access. Schools are likely to be protected by a 'firewall' from harmful internet sites, but adult supervision is usually going to be required as well.

There will be 'internet rules' along the following lines:

- I will never give out my home address, personal email address or telephone number or arrange to meet anyone over the internet.
- I will only use the internet and search engines when I have permission to do so.
- I will only email people that I know or who my teacher has approved and when I have been given permission.
- Any messages I send shall be polite, respectful and sensible.
- I understand that the use of chat rooms is not allowed under any circumstance.

- If I am uncomfortable or upset by anything I see on the internet I will immediately tell my teacher.
- I will not download files without my teacher's permission.
- I understand that the school can check my computer files and the internet sites I visit.

The policy should also expressly state equality of opportunity in accessing ICT along these lines: '*All children have access to the use of ICT regardless of gender, race, cultural background or physical or sensory disability.*' It should also make reference to health and safety aspects of using ICT, such as the following examples.

- Children shall not be responsible for moving heavy equipment around the school. They may load software but should not be given the responsibility of plugging in and switching machines on without a member of staff present.
- Food and drink may not be consumed near ICT equipment.
- It is the responsibility of staff to ensure that classroom ICT equipment is stored securely, cleaned regularly and that their class or themselves leave the ICT suite clean and tidy after use.
- Staff should ensure that children are seated at the computers comfortably and must be aware of the dangers of continuous use (e.g. eye/wrist strain).

To effectively support pupils in the use of ICT you need to be familiar yourself with the software and programs they are being asked to use. This means you should have practised with them first. Only when you are familiar with them can you explain to the pupils how to use them. This has obvious implications for planning and preparation. Part of your weekly timetable should include time for preparation, and good use can be made of this by practising on computers before working with the class.

How to select and use learning packages to match the age and development levels of the pupils with whom you work

Although the software used by pupils you support is likely to have been chosen by the teacher, part of your role is to monitor how effective that software is. It may be that, for some of the pupils you support, the loading process is too complex or the level of English used in it is too advanced for them to access independently. If you find this to be the case, you need to inform the class teacher. Discussion with the ICT manager or with the SENCO may give you some ideas about more appropriate software.

The scope of ICT skills needed by pupils and what can be expected from the age group with which you work

Using ICT is an integral part of education from the **Foundation Stage** onwards. Within the National Curriculum it is to be taught in its own right and used in most other subjects as well.

Foundation Stage

Children in Reception or Early Years will begin to use computers and programmable toys such as Roamers. They will begin to use appropriate vocabulary.

Key Stage 1

Children will use a range of ICT equipment both in literacy and numeracy. They will begin to learn the basics of word processing and use a variety of ways to present information.

Key Stage 2

Pupils will become more capable in the use of ICT and develop skills in working with a greater range of software, including word processing, audio-visual presentations and the internet. The aim is that using ICT becomes both natural and normal and can be applied in a variety of subjects.

Key Stages 3 and 4

Students are expected to develop knowledge of technical aspects of how ICT works. They need to become proficient in the use of multimedia presentations and to collaborate in presenting information in a wide range of formats. They are expected to develop a good understanding as to when using ICT is appropriate and when it is better to use something else.

How to support the development of ICT skills in pupils

You need to support pupils in ICT in line with the teacher's long-term and medium-term plans. Depending on the age of the pupils you will be helping them develop one or more of the following:

- Using basic computer skills – learning to turn on the computer, log on, use a mouse and keyboard.

Figure 11.1 Pupils need to be taught ICT skills

- Selecting and using appropriate software packages – under the guidance of the teacher, choosing packages which are 'fit for purpose', i.e. which do the job needed without undue complexity.
- Accessing and using learning programs – using CD-ROMs, the school intranet and the internet to access programs, using these programs as independently as possible.
- Accessing information – use all of the above knowledge to gain information for other subjects such as geography, history, science or RE.
- Using electronic communication systems – use the internet and communicate via email with increasing sophistication.

How to promote independence in the use of ICT equipment by pupils

When supporting pupils in ICT it is all too easy to do the work for them, particularly in the early stages. Your role is to tell them how to develop the skills they need and, where appropriate, model this for them. At all times you should encourage them to 'have a go' themselves and to develop their independent skills. You should remind them to continually save their work so it is not lost if something goes wrong.

Many pupils are more willing to experiment using ICT than when writing as they can edit errors out with ease. However, it is important to encourage them to keep records of their progress through saving work, even in the draft stages.

Risks associated with equipment and how to minimise them

All electrical and electronic equipment carries a certain amount of risk. It is the duty of the ICT manager or technician to ensure that all equipment is regularly checked and adequately maintained; however, all staff and pupils have a responsibility to be on the lookout for faulty wiring, unsafe cabling and so on. Any risk needs to be communicated to the appropriate persons as soon as possible. One way to minimise the risk of losing work or of damaging equipment is to ensure pupils always shut down their computers properly.

Checklist

✔ I know what ICT resources are in my school and where they are located.
✔ I am familiar with the procedures in my school for using these resources in class.
✔ I can safely and effectively operate all the ICT equipment in my school.
✔ I am familiar with the legislation regarding the use of ICT in schools.
✔ I am familiar with the school's ICT policy, particularly regarding the use of the internet.
✔ I am aware of the software available for use in my school and know which ones are most suitable for the pupils I work with.
✔ I know how to support pupils so they make progress in their ICT skills while developing both confidence and independence.

MEETING PERFORMANCE INDICATORS

3.17.1 Prepare ICT equipment for use in the classroom

Setting the scene

Mr Palmerston's Year 6 class are studying the Tudors in history and Miranda has been asked to support them in the ICT suite where they are to use the internet to help research information about Henry VIII. Prior to the lesson, her role is to ensure that the suite is available, that all the computers are running and are connected to the internet. During the lesson she is to be available to help any pupil with their research and to help them present their findings in a Word document.

Writing personal accounts: covering performance indicators

As evidence of her lesson input, Miranda could have written a personal account, but her assessor was coming to observe her. This is what he wrote up.

Observation Notes

Candidate: Miranda Appleton
School: Anywhere Primary School
Date: 2.5.06

3.17.1 Prepare ICT equipment for use in the classroom	*Performance indicators observed*
The lesson observed took place in the afternoon. Mr Palmerston told me that in the morning he had asked Miranda if she would ensure the computer suite was available at the time he wanted. She had therefore gone to the ICT suite, looked on the timetable, confirmed that the slot was free and had written the class name in to book it.	*Confirmed the requirements for ICT equipment with the teacher* *Checked the availability of the required ICT equipment*
My observation took place in the ICT suite. Just before the lesson was to begin, Miranda went into the suite to check that all the computers were working and were able to be logged on to the internet.	*Checked that the equipment was switched on, ready and safe for use when needed*
She found that two computers were not opening up properly. She confirmed that all the others were able to be logged on to the internet. She recorded the fact that two computers were not working in the technician's log book in the ICT suite and immediately reported this to Mr Palmerston when he brought the class into the suite. She turned the two computers off at the power supply.	*Ensured that any faulty equipment was isolated from any power source and made safe and secure*
As the computers are permanently set up in the ICT suite, she did not have to set them up. She did, however, check that they were properly connected to the printers and that the main computer was correctly linked to the suite's interactive whiteboard so that Mr Palmerston could demonstrate to the whole class what he wanted them to do.	*Made sure that there was ready access to accessories, consumables and information to use the equipment effectively*

Finally, Miranda ran a practice page through the printer to make sure there was adequate ink. She also checked to ensure there was a sufficient supply of paper for the lesson.

Made sure that there was ready access to accessories, consumables and information to use the equipment effectively

Signed: Terrie Cole

Terrie Cole
NVQ Assessor

3.17.2 Support classroom use of ICT equipment

Miranda's assessor was able to observe her meeting the performance indicators with regards to personal computers and peripherals. She will on other occasions need to have the other aspects of the scope of supporting the use of ICT equipment witnessed.

Unit 3.17.2 Support classroom use of ICT equipment

Performance indicators	*Scope*
(1) Operate *ICT equipment* correctly and safely when asked to do so.	(a) Overhead projection equipment (b) Recording and playback equipment (c) Personal computers and peripherals, including printers, modem links, software packages
(2) Give clear guidance and instructions on the use of *ICT equipment* by others.	(a) Overhead projection equipment (b) Recording and playback equipment (c) Personal computers and peripherals, including printers, modem links, software packages
(3) Give support as needed to help pupils develop *skills* in the use of ICT.	(a) Basic user skills (b) Selection and use of appropriate software packages (c) Accessing and using learning programmes (d) Accessing information (e) Using electronic communication systems
(4) Provide an appropriate level of assistance to enable pupils to experience a sense of achievement, maintain self-confidence and encourage self help skills in the use of ICT.	
(5) Monitor the safe use of *equipment* by others and intervene promptly where actions may be dangerous.	(a) Overhead projection equipment (b) Recording and playback equipment (c) Personal computers and peripherals, including printers, modem links, software packages
(6) Regularly check that *equipment* is working properly and promptly report any faults to the appropriate person.	(a) Overhead projection equipment (b) Recording and playback equipment (c) Personal computers and peripherals, including printers, modem links, software packages

(7) Use only approved accessories and consumables.	
(8) Make sure that the *equipment* is left in a safe condition after use.	(a) Overhead projection equipment (b) Recording and playback equipment (c) Personal computers and peripherals, including printers, modem links, software packages
(9) Make sure that the *equipment* is stored safely and securely after use.	(a) Overhead projection equipment (b) Recording and playback equipment (c) Personal computers and peripherals, including printers, modem links, software packages

Observation Notes

Candidate: Miranda Appleton
School: Anywhere Primary School
Date: 2.5.06

3.17.2 Support classroom use of ICT equipment

Performance indicators observed

Two pupils found it difficult to log on to the internet and, at Mr Palmerston's request, Miranda showed them how to do it. She performed the operation herself; then logged off so the pupils could do it for themselves.

Operated ICT equipment correctly and safely

Later in the lesson Mr Palmerston asked her to help another group of pupils print some of their work. Again she showed them how to make the appropriate operations using the keyboard and mouse; then they did it for themselves.

Gave clear guidance and instructions on the use of ICT equipment by others

All the pupils have had experience of using the internet, but not all of them could readily find relevant websites. Some found themselves looking at websites for Tudor-style houses for sale or Tudor-theme weekends. Miranda gave them tips on how to narrow their search and use search engines more effectively. She gave guidance as to how to judge which websites were likely to yield more relevant information.

Gave support as needed to help pupils develop skills in the use of ICT

Throughout the lesson Miranda was careful to promote pupil independence and confidence in using ICT. Even when asked, she never did the work for them. Most were familiar with what they were being asked to do, but about four or five struggled. Miranda encouraged them to 'have a go' and to make their own decisions as to which web sites to visit.

Provided an appropriate level of assistance to enable pupils to experience a sense of achievement, maintain self-confidence and encourage self-help skills in the use of ICT

The class teacher had paired some of these less confident pupils with others more familiar with the internet who could have dominated the partnership. As Miranda walked around the ICT suite she made sure that both pupils got equal 'shares' in operating the equipment so that those less familiar with it gained in confidence.

Monitored the safe use of equipment by others and intervened promptly where actions may be dangerous

Mostly, two pupils worked at each computer. While this meant that the class gained experience in collaborative working, there was also the possibility of disagreement and even argument. On three occasions during the lesson I observed

Miranda stepping in to defuse situations where one pupil was getting cross with his or her partner. She was clearly aware that it could become dangerous if one tried to snatch the mouse or the keyboard from the other.

During the lesson Miranda walked around the ICT suite looking at the screens, making sure that the computers continued to work properly.

Regularly checked that equipment was working properly

The only consumables used during the lesson were paper and printer ink.

Used only approved accessories and consumables

Towards the end of the lesson Miranda went round to each couple to make sure they were saving their work and closing the computer down properly.

Made sure that the equipment was left in a safe condition after use

At the end of the lesson Miranda placed the interactive whiteboard pens and eraser back in the lockable ICT cabinet in the head teacher's office. Every other piece of equipment used is secured in the ICT suite.

Made sure the equipment was stored safely and securely after use

At the end of the session the assessor asked Miranda a few questions to clarify some aspects of the lesson. This discussion contributes to the evidence for the performance indicators for this unit.

Assessor: Why did you turn the two computers off at the power supply when you discovered they were not working?

Miranda: Even though they weren't faulty as such, I wanted to be sure that they were safe so that, if a pupil did try to turn them on, nothing would happen.

(PI – ensure that any faulty equipment is isolated from any power source and made safe and secure)

Assessor: How did you know what you needed to do to ensure that the main computer was linked to the interactive whiteboard?

Miranda: I have been taught how to do this by the ICT technician. All this is in line with the maker's instructions.

(PI – Follow manufacturers and safety instructions for setting up the ICT equipment)

Assessor: How do you ensure that the consumables used in the lesson are approved?

Miranda: The consumables are supplied within the ICT suite and are approved by the school, being ordered by the ICT technician. I know not to bring anything into the suite which has not been approved.

(PI – Use only approved accessories and consumables)

Assessor's comments

I am very impressed with your level of knowledge and the skills you show when supporting pupils in ICT. I have spoken with Mr Palmerston, and he reports that you are a real asset to the class. Can you let me have a copy of what you wrote in the ICT technician's log book as evidence, please?

Signed: Terrie Cole

Terrie Cole
NVQ Assessor

After much hard work, Miranda, Nicola and Nazreen finally finish the course.

As they look at each other's portfolios they realise that though there are similar features in their portfolios there are also differences.

As Terrie Cole, their assessor, comments, there is no *one* right way to put together the evidence for an NVQ 2.

When their certificates finally arrived, Miranda, Nicola and Nazreen could be seen doing a victory dance (Figure 11.2).

Figure 11.2 Doing the Victory Dance

Chapter 12

National documents and strategies relating to SEN and inclusion

The Salamanca Statement (UNESCO 1994)

Like most countries in the world, the United Kingdom supports the Salamanca Statement. This statement, drawn up by a UNESCO world conference held in Salamanca, Spain in 1994, called upon all governments to '*adopt as a matter of law or policy the principle of inclusive education, enrolling all children in regular schools, unless there are compelling reasons for doing otherwise*'.

Government documents

A number of government documents (covering England and Wales) are listed in chronological order below.

Special Educational Needs: Report of the Committee of Enquiry into the Education of Handicapped Children and Young People (Warnock Report) (Department of Education and Science (DES) 1978)

The Warnock Report is the bedrock upon which all subsequent SEN strategy and legislation has been based. The report coined the phrase '*special educational need*' (SEN) and established the understanding of a '*continuum of need*' which required a corresponding '*continuum of provision*'.

At the heart of the Warnock Report was the belief that fundamental distinctions between children in the way they are educated are wrong: '*The purpose of education for all children is the same; the goals are the same*' (DES 1978: 5).

The report noted that the number of support staff in mainstream schools was growing in response to an increasing number of pupils with special needs being educated in mainstream schools.

Code of Practice on the Identification and Assessment of Special Educational Needs (Department for Education (DfE) 1994)

This document set the tone for special educational needs provision throughout the country. It was based upon the findings of the Warnock Report and every school had to 'have regard' to it. However, it only related to identification and assessment, it did not say *how* pupils with learning difficulties should be taught or *what* they should be taught, neither did it detail what the learning difficulties might be.

It stated that 20 per cent of pupils nationally are likely to have some degree of SEN (statistics linked to Warnock). The majority of this need will be met by the school, with outside help where appropriate. However, the proportion of children with SEN will vary significantly from area to area.

The Code established the principle that pupils with learning difficulties need to be identified and assessed early. The earlier action is taken, the more responsive the child is likely to be. It also stated that children have a right to be heard and should be encouraged to take part in the decision making process.

The Code introduced a five-staged approach to SEN provision which recognised there is a continuum of SEN (the phrase used by Warnock). The majority of children with SEN will have their needs met by stages 1–3, perhaps 2 per cent will need to move to Stages 4 or 5 (the statementing process).

Excellence for All Children: Meeting Special Educational Needs (Department for Education and Employment (DfEE) 1997)

This consultative document was produced by the newly elected Labour government to establish its commitment to inclusion: '*By inclusion we mean not only that pupils with SEN should wherever possible receive their education in mainstream school, but also that they should join fully with their peers in the curriculum and life of the school.*'

A Programme for Action: Meeting Special Educational Needs (DfEE 1998)

This followed the consultation document *Excellence for All Children* (DfEE 1997) and looked at ways of fostering inclusion by considering a range of issues in SEN practice. It led directly to the publication of the revised Code of Practice which was first issued in draft form in July 2000 and was implemented in January 2001.

Social Inclusion: Pupil Support (DfEE 1999, Circular 10/99)

This document identified groups of pupils at particular risk of disaffection and social exclusion. For pupils at risk of permanent exclusion, pastoral support programmes (PSPs) are to be set up by the school and relevant agencies, which could include social services, housing, careers services, community and voluntary groups. Educational psychologists and behavioural support teams are likely to be involved.

The National Curriculum (Curriculum 2000) Inclusion Statement (Qualifications and Curriculum Authority (QCA) and DfEE 2000)

Curriculum 2000 aimed to provide a more inclusive framework than previous versions of the National Curriculum:

> This National Curriculum includes for the first time a detailed, overarching statement on inclusion which makes clear the principles schools must follow in

> their teaching right across the curriculum, to ensure that all pupils have the chance to succeed, whatever their individual needs and the potential barriers to their learning may be . . . Equality of opportunity is one of a broad set of common values and purposes which underpins the school curriculum and the work of schools.

In planning and teaching the National Curriculum, teachers are required to have 'due regard' to the following principles:

1 setting appropriate challenges
2 providing for the diversity of pupils' needs
3 providing for pupils with SEN
4 providing support for pupils for whom English is an additional language.

Working with Teaching Assistants: A Good Practice Guide (DfEE 2000)

This document was distributed to all schools in the form of a ring binder. Provided mainly for head teachers and managers, it was part of the government's strategy to improve the lot of teaching assistants in schools across the country. However, it also provides valuable information for teaching assistants as it looks at their role in school and gives guidance on how they may best be deployed and managed. It does not, however, deal with issues of pay and grading, explicitly stating that the government believes this is best left for negotiation at the local level. This document fixed the use of the term 'Teaching Assistant' to cover roles that had previously been described by a variety of terms.

Special Educational Needs Code of Practice (DfEE 2001)

All schools 'must have regard to' this Code of Practice, which supersedes the Code of Practice of 1994. This Code develops two principles more fully than previous documents:

- partnership with parents
- pupil participation.

It identifies four main categories of special need – cognition and skills for learning, physical and sensory impairments, social and communication interaction difficulties and emotional and behavioural difficulties.

The staged approach

The Code of Practice recognises that there is no distinct 'cut-off' between children with SEN and those without. Every school should have in place stages relating to degrees of provision. The Code of Practice describes these stages as Early Identification (EI), School Action (SA) and School Action Plus (SA+), with slightly different terminology being used for the Early Years.

Early Identification is the most basic level of intervention and occurs when a class teacher identifies a child as experiencing a measure of difficulty in school. Intervention at this stage is organised by the class teacher within the class using resources generally available.

At *School Action* the class teacher identifies a pupil experiencing SEN and devises interventions *additional to* or *different from* those provided as part of the school's usual curriculum. The class teacher and SENCO are jointly responsible for drawing up a programme of intervention. They will write an Individual Education Plan which specifies targets for that pupil and outlines what provision will be put in place to meet those targets. The IEP should only record that which is *additional to* or *different from* the differentiated curriculum plan, which is in place as part of the provision for all children. IEPs should be reviewed at least twice a year.

The highest level of intervention within school is *School Action Plus*, when the school, in consultation with parents, asks for help from external services such as educational psychologists.

Statements of Special Educational Need

If a child's needs are so severe or complex that provision at School Action or School Action Plus will not be sufficient, or, if a child has been supported at those stages and has still made little or no progress over a period of time, then consideration may be given to providing that child with a *Statement of Special Educational Need*. This is a legal document which sets out the needs of a child and the provision to be made for that child by a local authority which has to be reviewed at least annually.

Supporting the Target Setting Process (QCA/DfEE 2001)

This provides guidance on target-setting for pupils with special educational needs who are working towards Level 1 in the National Curriculum by setting out for English, maths and science finely graded attainments known as the 'P Scales' ('Performance Scales').

Removing Barriers to Achievement: The Government's Strategy for SEN (Department for Education and Skills (DfES) 2004)

This sets out the government's strategy for the education of children with special needs and disabilities. The key areas are early intervention, removing barriers to learning, raising expectations and achievements, and delivering improvements in partnerships.

Every Child Matters: Change for Children (DfES 2004)

The consultative Green Paper *Every Child Matters* was published by the government in 2003 alongside the report into the death of Victoria Climbié, seeking to strengthen services preventing the abuse of children. It focused on four themes:

- Supporting families and carers.
- Ensuring appropriate intervention takes place so that vulnerable children do not 'fall through the net'.

- Improving the accountability of all children's services and seeking to promote their inter-working.
- Ensuring that people working with children are valued, rewarded and trained.

Following the consultation, Parliament passed the Children Act 2004 and published *Every Child Matters: Change for Children* in November 2004. This is described as '*a new approach to the well-being of children and young people from birth to age 19*'. (www.everychildmatters.gov.uk/aims/ updated on 20 March 2006).

Every organisation involved with providing services for children is to work together, share information and develop networks so that every child, whatever their background or their circumstances benefits from the government's stated 'five outcomes':

- Be healthy.
- Stay safe.
- Enjoy and achieve.
- Make a positive contribution.
- Achieve economic well-being.

As part of their strategy to meet these objectives, the government has established a Children's Commissioner for England and is in the process of creating Children's Trusts throughout the country. Extended schools and the Common Assessment Framework (CAF) also form part of this strategy.

For children with special needs, Children's Trusts are to ensure:

- Effective delegation of resources to support early intervention and inclusion.
- Reduced reliance on SEN statements.
- Appropriate provision.
- Better specialist advice and support to schools and information to parents.
- A reduction in bureaucracy.

This is in line with the government strategy set out in *Removing Barriers to Achievement* (www.everychildmatters.gov.uk/ete/sen updated 10 May 2005, accessed 20 March 2006).

Local authorities were required to produce a three-year children and young people's plan from April 2006 which will be a single plan shared between all children's services.

Workforce Reform: the National Agreement (2003)

(www.remodelling.org/remodelling/nationalagreement.aspx)
In order to reduce teacher workload (and thereby improve 'work–life balance') and to raise standards in schools a National Agreement was signed by government, employers and trade unions in January 2003. Under this, routine administration tasks have been removed from teachers and given to support staff and guaranteed professional time for planning, preparation and assessment (PPA) has been introduced.

The National Agreement recognises that support staff have a crucial role to play in Workforce Remodelling and led directly to the establishment of Higher Level Teaching Assistants (HLTA). The government is also developing nationwide strategies to improve training and career possibilities for all support staff. The Teacher Training Agency

(TTA) has now become the Training and Development Agency for Schools (TDA) and for the first time includes training for support staff as well as teachers. This body also now oversees the work previously undertaken by the National Remodelling Team.

Obtainable via the Local Government Employers' website (www.lge.gov.uk) the document *School Support Staff – The Way Forward* (Employers' Organisation for local government/GMB/T&G/UNISON 2003) outlines national guidance containing model job profiles, employment good practice and advice on training and development of school support staff which has been agreed by the National Joint Council (NJC) for Local Government Services. It may be worth noting that if you go to the above website and search for 'TA' you will get something on military service!

Further information on the government's strategy for training and developing support staff can be found in the document *Developing People to Support Learning: A Skills Strategy for the Wider School Workforce 2006–2009* (TDA 2006) (www.tda.gov.uk).

Chapter 13

Legislation relating to SEN and inclusion in England and Wales

Major Education Acts

Education Act (England and Wales) 1944

- Local education authorities (LEAs) must meet the needs of all handicapped children (classified into a number of categories such as blind pupils, educationally subnormal pupils, epileptic pupils, maladjusted pupils, delicate pupils).
- Less seriously handicapped children might be educated in ordinary schools.
- Those with severe disabilities should be educated in special schools.
- Any child considered to be educable must have access to schooling as of right.
- Parents are required to submit their children for medical examination.
- No specific provision made for parents to appeal against LEA decision that their child required special education.

Education (Handicapped Children) Act 1970

- LEAs rather than health authorities given responsibility for the education of 'mentally handicapped' children.
- About 400 new special schools were formed.

Education Act 1976

LEAs required to arrange for the special education of all handicapped pupils to be given in county and voluntary schools, except where this was impractical, incompatible with the efficient instruction in the schools or involved unreasonable public expenditure, in which case it could be given in special schools or in independent schools with the approval of the Secretary of State.

Education Act 1981

- 'Medical model' of need (i.e. there is something 'wrong' with the child) replaced by a more 'social model' (i.e. need is created by inappropriate environments).
- Enshrined the term *special educational need* within educational legislation – covers pupils who would previously have been in special schools and those who would have been in special or 'remedial' classes within mainstream schools.

- Defined 'special educational need' up to the present day. Children have a learning difficulty if they
    - have a significantly greater difficulty in learning than the majority of children of the same age; or
    - have a disability which prevents or hinders them from making use of educational facilities of a kind generally provided for children of the same age in schools within the area of the local education authority.
- Parents given new rights.

Education policy from this Act on has been to encourage schools to include those pupils who previously would have attended special schools. The implementation of this Act led to a rapid rise in the number of support staff being employed in schools.

Education Reform Act 1988

This Act introduced far-reaching and long-lasting changes for education:

- The National Curriculum ensured that all pupils share the same statutory entitlement to a 'broad balanced curriculum'.
- Local management of schools (LMS) meant that schools rather than LEAs were responsible for managing funding and for the quality of education for all their pupils.

For the first time it was laid down in law that schools were to provide a common curriculum for all children.

Education Act 1993

Children with special educational needs should – where this is what the parents want – normally be educated at mainstream schools. The Act enshrined this principle in law for the first time. However, pupils and their families had to satisfy a series of conditions. The Act also set up the SEN tribunal system under which parents could appeal against certain decisions made by the LEA in the statementing process.

Education Act 1996

- Consolidated the Education Act 1993.
- LEAs have a general duty to educate children who have special educational needs in a mainstream school if that is what parents want.
- The governing body of every maintained school must ensure the following:
    - Teachers are aware of children's SEN.
    - The necessary provision is made for any pupil who has SEN.
    - Children with SEN join in the activities of the school with their peers as far as is 'reasonably practicable'.
- Schools should appoint a SEN governor, however, the responsibility for SEN provision remains with the full governing body as a 'whole-school issue'.

- Governors, with the head teacher, are required under the Act to
  - develop a whole-school policy for SEN
  - publish it in the school prospectus
  - inform parents about the success of the policy in the governor's annual report.

Education Act 2002

Schools are required to offer extended services to their local communities, but before they do so they must consult with pupils, staff, parents and carers, local communities and the local authority. Such consultation should be carried out regularly to ensure that what is offered via extended school is what the community needs.

The aim is that, by 2010, all children should have access to a variety of extended services in or through their school in line with the *Every Child Matters* agenda. Children with disabilities and/or special educational needs must be able to access all extended services.

Support staff, if they choose, may well be involved in providing some of these extended services.

The Act also sets out the circumstances in which aspects of teaching roles can be performed by staff other than teachers in line with Workforce Remodelling. This relates to all staff other than teachers and not simply HLTAs.

Other Legislation

Health and Safety at Work Act 1974

This is the overarching legislation covering health and safety policies, and all school polices must relate to it. Every school must produce a plan for Health and Safety to ensure that hazards are assessed and the necessary arrangements are made to avoid or control risks.

Each employee in the school has a responsibility to '*take reasonable care for the health and safety of himself/herself, and of other persons who may be affected by his/her omissions at work*'. This includes making sure that all clothing complies with health and safety legislation – you are legally obliged to wear suitable clothing and shoes which do not slip.

Under the Act, it is illegal for a member of staff to take no action if they spot a potential danger. All staff are required by law to ensure that their actions do not put others at risk. This includes tidying up materials and putting things away after use.

The Children Act 1989

- Enshrines in law the principle that the interest of the child must always be put first.
- Children should be involved in all that happens to them – their views must be ascertained and taken into account by those working with them.
- All staff are required to protect children against risk and danger.
- Appropriate safety equipment must be used and worn at all times and any tools and equipment being used by pupils must be designed for the job in hand and be in good condition. It is the responsibility of all staff to ensure this is the case.
- Regulates child protection matters, particularly how disclosures should be responded to. Members of staff have a legal duty to report any concerns and suspicions.

Management of Health and Safety Regulations 1992

Stipulate that schools must draw up arrangements for health and safety following regular risk assessments. Included in this are issues such as security in school, supervision of children, children and staff records or data, Child Protection and Health and Safety in the National Curriculum.

Disability Discrimination Act 1995

- Duty '*not to discriminate against disabled pupils and prospective pupils in the provision of education and associated services in schools, and in respect of admissions and exclusions*'.
- Duty to plan for increased accessibility – '*wherever possible disabled people should have the same opportunities as non-disabled people in their access to education*'.
- Based upon a Social Model of disability
  - recognises difference and diversity within the community
  - sees the potential problems as within the environment *not* within the person
  - need to identify *barriers* to be overcome
  - a disability is a handicap only if the environment makes it so.

Data Protection Act 1998

The aim of the Data Protection Act is to protect the rights of the individual by ensuring that any information kept is accurate and is protected. This legislation applies to records kept on pupils in schools.

There are eight basic principles to the Act:

1. Information must be obtained and processed legally.
2. Data should be held only for specific purposes.
3. Personal data held for a purpose must not be disclosed in a manner incompatible with that purpose.
4. Personal data held should be accurate and not excessive.
5. Personal data should be accurate and up to date.
6. Personal data should not be kept longer than necessary.
7. An individual should have access to their records.
8. Appropriate security measures should protect the data.

Schools need to make individual records available to the appropriate parents as well as pupils; keep attendance and academic records only as long as they are relevant; and ensure that all records are stored securely, whether they be paper records or computerised.

Computers with pupil records on must not be left unattended in public places. They must not be positioned where people can read the screen. Screen saver passwords must be used which must be kept secret. Back-up copies of records must be systematically made.

Paper records must be stored in a secure cabinet or area; they must not be left lying around anywhere.

Disposal of records must be undertaken with care – shredding is recommended. They must not simply be placed in waste paper baskets.

Race Relations (Amendment) Act 2000

Having its origins in the report following the murder of Stephen Lawrence in 1993, this Act built on the regulations laid down by the Race Relations Act 1976. It made it incumbent upon all public bodies, including schools, not only to work against racial discrimination and address racial harassment, but also to actively promote racial equality and good race relations. This applies to staff, parents and pupils alike.

Special Educational Needs and Disability Act (SENDA) 2001

This Act states that public bodies (including schools) need to take account of the Disability Discrimination Act 1995. In so doing it gave legal 'teeth' to some of the provisions in the revised Code of Practice (2001):

- Schools have a legal obligation not to discriminate against pupils who have disabilities and to make all possible provision for their needs.
- The right to a mainstream education for children with special educational needs is strengthened both for pupils with statements and those without.
- Where parents want a mainstream education for their child everything possible should be done to provide it. Equally where the parents of pupils who have statements want a special school place their wishes should be listened to and taken into account.
- Mainstream education cannot be refused on the grounds that the child's needs cannot be provided for within the mainstream sector.

The Children Act 2004

This Act provides the legal underpinning for the government's initiative *Every Child Matters: Change for Children* with its 'five outcomes':

- Be healthy.
- Stay safe.
- Enjoy and achieve.
- Make a positive contribution.
- Achieve economic well-being.

Every school must be working towards these five outcomes.

Local authorities are required to ensure the delivery of extended services in or through schools. They are required to create children's services directorates, publish children and young people's plans and to identify a lead member for children's services. They must also take measures to ensure that 'swift and easy referral' to specialist services for those pupils who require such provision is available through all schools by 2010.

Freedom of Information Act 2000

This Act came into force for schools January 2005.

Schools are legally obliged to produce a 'publication scheme' which sets out the type of information published by the school, how it will be published and whether it is free or not. Anyone has the right to request information from schools, however, only those with *bona fide* reasons can be granted access to personal records. Such records continue to be covered by the Data Protection Act and come under the category of 'Absolute Exemptions' to the Freedom of Information Act.

Disability Discrimination Act 2005

- Adds to DDA 1995 and SENDA 2001, does not supersede them.
- Duty to promote disability equality – the 'general duty' on public bodies.
- Duty on the 'responsible body' (for schools this is the governors) to '*take such steps as it is reasonable to take to ensure that disabled pupils are not placed at a substantial disadvantage*'.
- Duty to prepare a Disability Equality Scheme – an action plan detailing the steps that the 'responsible body' will take to fulfil its obligations.
- Primary schools have to have this in place by December 2007.
- Requirement to involve disabled people in its development.

Appendices

PHOTOCOPIABLE TEMPLATES FOR PERFORMANCE INDICATORS OR EVIDENCE OF KNOWLEDGE BASE

2.1.1 Help with organisation of the learning environment

Checking the availability of safety equipment

What can be found in a first aid box?

Equipment	*Seen*	*Comments*	*Witnessed by*
Scissors			
Guidance Card			
Safety pins			
Disposable gloves			
Sterile coverings			
Individual sterile dressings			
Cloth triangular bandage			
Medium dressings			
Large dressings			
Eye pad			

2.1.1 Help with organisation of the learning environment

The learning resources and materials

Learning environment	*Seen*	*Worked in*	*Witness*
All the classrooms			
Hall			
ICT area			
Science area			
Cooking area			
Playground			
Environmental area			
Outdoor games area			
Music area			
Art area			
Design and technology area			
Areas for additional teaching (small groups, booster classes and so on)			
Other (specify)			

Resources	*Seen*	*Used*	*Witness*
General stock cupboard			
ICT – software and hardware			
Maths			
Literacy			
Science, including environmental resources			
Design and technology			
Art			
Music			
PE			
History			
Geography			
RE			
PSHSE			
Local studies			
Other (specify)			

2.1.2 Help with the keeping of records

Record keeping in the school

Member of staff	*Responsibilities for record keeping*
Administration officer	
School secretary	
Head teacher	
Deputy head teacher	
Head of year	
Subject managers	
Classroom teachers	
SENCO	
Ethnic minority manager	
Gifted and talented manager	
Caretaker	
Others (specify)	

2.2.1 Help with the care and support of individual pupils

Difficulties that might arise in interacting effectively with a pupil and how to deal with these	*Ways that I could deal with these*
Pupils who always want me to do the work for them.	
Pupils who find it difficult to pay attention.	
Pupils who always want to have things their way.	
Pupils who feel they are not as good as other pupils.	
Pupils who make fun of other pupils that are struggling with their work.	
Pupils who refuse to do what I ask them.	

2.3 Provide support for learning activities

Problems that might occur in supporting learning	*Possible explanations*	*Strategies that can be used to support learning*
Pupils may find the task too difficult.		
Pupils may not understand the task.		
Pupils may say they are bored and they don't want to do the task.		
One pupil may not want to join in.		
Pupils may not be paying attention.		
A pupil may say that they are stupid and that they cannot do a task.		
Pupils might be distracted by other activities.		
They might persistently ask when it is time for break or when it is time for lunch.		
One pupil always wants to dominate the group.		
One pupil who likes to criticise other pupils.		
Having several needy pupils fighting for your attention.		
When playing a game the pupil who always wants to go first.		
When playing a game the pupil who finds it hard to lose.		

3.1 Contribute to the management of pupil behaviour

Routine	*School and class rules*	*Role and responsibility of yourselves and others*			
	Pupils are expected to	*I (the TA) will intervene when*	*I (the TA) can use these strategies*	*I (the TA) will inform the teacher*	*The teacher will*
In the playground					
Standing outside in the corridor waiting to come into class					
Beginning of the day					
Where to sit					
When wishing to participate in class					
When requesting help					
Going into assembly					
Walking in corridors					
Using ICT equipment					

INDIVIDUAL EDUCATION PLANS

ANYWHERE PRIMARY SCHOOL INDIVIDUAL EDUCATION PLAN

Name:	Date of birth:
Class/year:	IEP no:
Male/Female:	Stage:
EAL: Y/N	First drawn up:
Summary of concern:	
Medical condition:	
Review dates:	Present:
External agencies:	
Comments:	Actions:

Targets	Success criteria	Possible resources	Possible strategies	Outcomes
Start date:				Date:
1.				
2.				
3.				

ASSESSMENT RESULTS, PROVISION AND EXTERNAL AGENCY COMMENTS	NOTES/PARENTAL CONTACT
Dyslexia Screening Tests (name of assessment):	
Reading (name and date of test):	
Spelling (name and date of test):	
Maths (name and date of test):	
Provision	
External agencies	

Example of IEP targets

Targets	Success criteria	Possible resources	Possible strategies	Outcomes
Start date: Jan 2006				Date: March 2006
1. To read and spell words with the long vowel phonemes *ai/ ee/ ea/ oo*	Pupil reads and spells a selection of these words accurately on five occasions	Plastic letters, worksheets, phonic books and CDs, phonic cards	Play games such as pairs, complete worksheets, listen to pupil read and focus on these phonic patterns	
2. To use the above spelling rules in own writing	Pupil uses spelling rules being worked on in five pieces of independent writing	Spelling banks, prompt cards	Make sure pupil under-stands the spelling rules, talk through written work with pupil focus-ing on the rule	
3. To listen to and follow instructions that have been given by an adult to the whole class	Over a period of one week 75% of instructions are followed within one minute of them being given	Target sheet, behaviour star chart, reward stickers	Make sure expectations of this behaviour are clearly understood and that pupil is aware of this target. Praise when achieved. Remind when missed.	

INDIVIDUAL BEHAVIOUR PLANS

ANYWHERE PRIMARY SCHOOL
INDIVIDUAL BEHAVIOUR PLAN

SECTION 1

Name of pupil: ____________________DOB: __________

Class teacher: ______________________________

NC Year: _____________

Name of Parent(s)/Carer(s): _________________________

Nominated person responsible for operating the plan:

____

Start date of plan, as agreed with parents and pupil:

____

Review dates:
- mid point: _____________
- end: _______________

External agencies (where applicable): _________________________

Persons contributing to the plan:

Name	*Contact no./address*

SECTION 2

Approaches/Behaviour causing concern

1.

2.

3.

Pupil's strengths

Desirable alternative behaviours (long term goals)

1.

2.

3.

Short term targets	Success criteria
1.	1.
2.	2.
3.	3.

SECTION 3

Strategies to support pupil

-
-
-

Special arrangements to be made

-
-
-

Support to be offered to help the pupil

Home:

Other agencies:

Rewards:

Home:

School:

Agreed consequences

-
-
-

SECTION 4

Review arrangements

Distribution list

Form completed by

Name: ______________________________

Designation: __________________________

Signature ....

CONFIDENTIAL: *for monitoring purposes only*
Number of fixed term exclusions this academic year and total days:

Is the child on the Child Protection Register? YES/NO
Is the child in public care? YES/NO

If YES
Accommodated by Local Authority? YES/NO
Subject of an interim or full care order? YES/NO
Subject of a supervision order? YES/NO

Ethnic origin: ______________________

First language: ______________________

ANYWHERE PRIMARY SCHOOL
INDIVIDUAL BEHAVIOUR PLAN
REVIEW MEETING

Name of pupil: ______________________ DOB: _______

Class: _________________________ NC Year: _________

Name of Parent(s)/Carer(s): ________________________

Date of initial behaviour plan: __________

Review No: _______

Date of review meeting: _____________ Time: _________
Venue:
Attended by:

Apologies from:

Summary of progress since the last meeting:

Agreed action:

1.

2.

3.

Arrangements for next review meeting: _____________ at _________ in school

Agreed circulation for this review form: __________________

Template for self-appraisal for teaching assistants

Name: Position:	
What I feel have been the key tasks/responsibilities of my job in relation to: • Supporting the school • Supporting the pupils • Supporting my colleagues • Supporting the curriculum	
Aspects of my work I'm most pleased with and why	
Aspects of my work I would like to improve and why	
Things preventing me working as effectively as I would like	
Changes I feel would improve my effectiveness	
My key aims for next year	
Training I would like to have	
How I would like my career to develop	
Signed	Date

Template for appraisal with teaching assistants

Name of TA: ______________________________

Name of appraiser: __________________________

Date of current appraisal: ______________________

Date of previous appraisal (where applicable): ______________

Targets set at last appraisal (where applicable)	Outcomes
1.	1.
2.	2.
3.	3.

Achievements over the past year with regard to:
(i.e. what has gone well, what the TA is most pleased with)

Support for pupils

Support for the teacher(s)

Support for the school

Training received by the TA over the past year

Type of training received (with dates)	Summary of what was learnt

---

Impact on what the TA does	Further considerations

Areas for development
(i.e. what may not have gone so well or what needs to be learnt/taken on board)

Support for pupils

Support for the teacher(s)

Support for the school

Career aspirations and possibilities

Targets for the next year

1.

2.

3.

Action to be taken

What action?	By whom?	By when?
1.		
2.		
3.		

Date for next appraisal:

Signed:

TA ______________________________

Appraiser ______________________________

FEEDBACK

Possible template of feedback form to teachers

NAME OF SCHOOL:

FEEDBACK FORM TO TEACHERS

Name of Teaching Assistant:	Date:
Names of pupils:	Resources used:
Learning objective(s):	Overall levels of achievement (1–5 where 1 is not at all and 5 is totally achieved):
Comments about any individual pupil or particular aspects of the activity:	

Signature of TA: ____________________ Date: ________

PERSONAL ACCOUNTS

Template for personal account (version 1)

NAME:
DATE:
ACTIVITY:
WHO WAS INVOLVED

What happened

Evaluation

Teacher's comments

I certify that this is a true statement of what occurred.

Teacher's signature

Name (printed and role)

Template for personal account (version 2)

NAME:
DATE:
ACTIVITY:
WHO WAS INVOLVED

Obtained information from the class teacher on the learning objectives of the activity.

Description of activity

Provided the teacher with relevant feedback

What went well:

What I was not happy with:

What I would do differently next time:

Teacher's comments

I certify that this is a true statement of what occurred.

Teacher's signature

Name (printed and role)

MATCHING EXERCISES

Matching exercise for Unit 3.1 Contribute to the management of pupil behaviour

As we have seen throughout this book there is a real art to writing personal accounts. What follows are three different versions of the **same event**.

Account 1: description

While I was walking down the corridor, 5 minutes after the start of the last lesson of the day, I met Jocelyn S. walking in the opposite direction crying. As Jocelyn is one of the students I support, I asked her what the problem was and she reported that she was looking for the Head of Year. I told her that the Head of Year was in a meeting and asked if I could help. She started to cry even more and said that one of the girls in her English Class had called her a slag and now all the girls were joining in. She said this had been going on for several weeks and that she could just not face going into a classroom with them again. I took Jocelyn to the classroom where she should have been and went inside to explain to the teacher why she was not there, leaving Jocelyn outside. I tactfully suggested to the teacher that as Jocelyn was so upset I take Jocelyn to the Learning Support Unit for the rest of the lesson. The teacher thought that was a good idea and gave me some work for Jocelyn to do. I took Jocelyn to the Learning Support Unit and told her that the school had an Anti-Bullying Policy and that the girls would be spoken to. Jocelyn was a much happier girl when she left the school at the end of the day. I then informed her Head of Year and her tutor. They both agreed to deal with it.

Account 2: description

I met J.S. walking in the opposite direction crying. J.S. said that she had a problem with other girls bullying her. I stepped in and sorted the problem and talked to the relevant people involved, in doing this I recognised when pupil behaviour conflicts with school policy and I responded promptly in line with my role and responsibility.

Account 3: description

While I was walking down the corridor, 5 minutes after the start of the last lesson of the day, I met J.S. walking in the opposite direction crying. J.S. said that one of the girls in her English Class had called her a slag and now all the girls were joining in. She said this had been going on for several weeks and that she could just not face going into a classroom with them again. As J.S. was so upset the English teacher (Miss L) gave me some work for J.S. and I went to the Learning Support Unit with her. At the Learning Support Unit the Anti-Bullying Policy was discussed with J.S.

Questions

1 In the various accounts – make a note of what performance indicators are covered. (Hint – underline the key phrases that prove that a performance indicator has been met)
2 How well do you think the personal accounts meet the performance indicators?
3 Would you include any other details in the accounts?
4 If you were the teaching assistant who would you get to witness the event?
5 Are there any issues regarding confidentiality?

Half-termly planning | Literacy | Year 3 | Spring Term 2006 (First half term)

Phonics, spelling and vocabulary	***Grammar and punctuation***	***Comprehension and composition***	***Texts***	***Week***
Continuous work Identify mis-spelt words in own writing; keep individual lists and learn to spell them Use independent spelling strategies, including sounding out and spelling using phonemes Practise new spellings regularly by 'look, say, cover, write, check'	**Continuous work**	**Continuous work**	**Range:**	
Blocked work Investigate and identify basic rules for changing the spelling of nouns when *s* is added Practise correct formation of diagonal joins to letters without ascenders Investigate, spell and read words with silent letters Practise correct formation of horizontal joins to letters without ascenders	**Blocked work** Extend knowledge and understanding of pluralisation – recognise singular and plural forms in speech and shared reading; transform sentences from singular to plural and *vice versa*	**Blocked work** Investigate the styles and voices of traditional story language e.g. *once upon a time . . .* – list, compare and use in own writing Recognise the importance of correct sequence – use writing frames for support	Traditional stories	1

Spelling strategies	**Blocked work**	**Blocked work**		
Using visual skills to spell words e.g. recognising common letter strings	Understand the function of adjectives within sentences	Identify and discuss main and recurring characters, evaluate their behaviour and justify views	Fables	2
Use apostrophe to spell shortened forms of words	Note where commas occur in reading and how they help the reader	Write a story plan for own myth, fable or traditional tale using story theme from reading but substituting different characters or changing the setting		
Investigate and identify basic rules for changing the spelling of nouns when *s* is added	Uses of capitilisation from reading – names, headings	Identify the different purposes of instructional texts e.g. recipes	Instructional texts	3
Use the terms 'singular' and 'plural' appropriately	Understand the term 'collective noun' and collect examples	Understand how written instructions are organised e.g. lists		
Recognise and spell common suffixes and how these influence word meanings e.g. *–ly*, *-ful*, *-ness*	Use terms 'singular' and 'plural' appropriately	Write instructions		
Spell by analogy with other know words e.g. *light*, *right*	Experiment with deleting words in sentences to see which are essential to retain meaning and which are not	Choose and prepare poems for performance	Poems to perform	4
		Identify typical story themes	Legends	5
		Write portraits of characters from story texts		
		Learn to make clear notes	Instructional texts	6

Literacy weekly planner for unit/module: But Martin

Date: Week beginning 6.9.06 Year group: 3

Objectives:

Text:	***Sentence:***	***Word:***	***Speaking and listening:***
For pupils to express their views about a story To generate ideas relevant to a topic by brainstorming and word association	To identify the function of verbs in sentences through 1) collecting and classifying examples of verbs from reading and own knowledge and 2) experimenting with changing simple verbs in sentences and discussing their impact on meaning	To demarcate the end of a sentence with a full stop and the start of a new one with a capital letter.	To describe their work

	Whole class	*Whole class*	*Remember to's*	*Independent task*	*Plenary*
Monday	Read the story 'But Martin' Discuss what the story is about Sequence key ideas on board	Discuss how pupils felt on their first day at school Introduce how to make name monsters	Aim: to make a name monster RT: use capital letters Have the fold at the bottom Make letters the size of the paper Don't cut off the letters	Make the name monster	What are our monsters like? Short verbal descriptions, compare and describe
Tuesday	Look at an example of a name monster Model writing a description of a name monster	Think about what the name monster looks like – age, size, what it eats, personality	Aim: to write a description of the name monster RT: use capital letters and full stops correctly Use interesting describing words	Children write about their monster	Listen to some examples Teach children how to highlight RTs Teacher to look at the marking to develop a response point e.g. misuse of capital letters
Wednesday	Imagine you are an alien and you have visited the school Discuss how different our school is to Martin's Recap experiences	Model the beginning of a broadcast, writing and performing in 'alien-like' voice	Aim: to write a radio broadcast RT: use capital letters and full stops	Children to write and then perform their description How Martin found the school	Listen to a few broadcasts Children to identify their favourite part

	that Martin had				
Thursday	Focus on page 13–19 of the book Identify the verbs and their purpose Try substituting different verbs and discuss the effects	Act a few suggestions out	Aim: Recognise and replace verbs RT: Choose different verbs	In groups of 6, children rewrite pages 13–19 (one page each group) using different verbs Act out this work	Perform and evaluate which were the best verbs
Friday	Recap the story of 'But Martin' What was their favourite part? Did they enjoy the story? Which parts and why?	Why have we read the story to you? What could you learn from it?	Aim: To review the story RT: complete the review sheet with own ideas	Children to complete 'But Martin' review sheet	Read some reviews Did we all like the same part? Discuss. Glue sheets into literacy books.

Literacy weekly planner for unit/module: But Martin

Date: Week beginning 6.9.06   Year group: 3

Curriculum targets: *To use capital letters and full stops; To recognise verbs; To use adjectives in a written description*

Class Reader: *But Martin*

Use of additional adults (TAs):

Monday	**Tuesday**	**Wednesday**	**Thursday**	**Friday**
General support in class as a whole, making sure all understand task and can respond to it; support as needed	Mainly stay with lower ability group help with spelling, ideas, punctuation	General support in class (as Monday)	Mainly stay with lower ability group helping them achieve learning objective	General support in the class

ICT:

Monday	**Tuesday**	**Wednesday**	**Thursday**	**Friday**
Interactive whiteboard – pages from 'But Martin' loaded on Write key ideas on interactive whiteboard	Model description already written on laptop and then displayed on interactive white board Three pupils use class computers for their independent work	Tape recording of a radio broadcast made by teachers Two groups can tape their performance	Use interactive whiteboard and pens to highlight verbs in the example page Involve children in doing this	Three more pupils can use class computers to write their reviews using the form on the hard drive

Homework:

Design own homework folder cover – must include child's name, class and the words 'Homework Folder'.

Assessment/evaluation:

Through discussion with pupils – marking of written work by teacher and TAs relating to the remember to's. Pupil assessment via their review sheets.

LEVEL 2 VQ: HOW KNOWLEDGE REQUIRED IN MANDATORY UNITS CAN BE MAPPED ONTO INFORMATION IN THIS TEXTBOOK

Support work in schools qualifications (SWiS VQs) are courses designed for all support staff to include: learning support, technicians, admistration/clerical/reception staff, cover supervisors, midday supervisors, after school supervisors and caretakers. To gain a **Level 2 VQ** support staff will need to complete two mandatory units and depending on the level of the qualification (award or certificate) choose to complete one or two optional units relevant to their field of work.

What follows is an outline of how the knowledge required for the Level 2 mandatory units can be mapped onto the information in this textbook. As this is a textbook written for teaching assistants the information presented in this book will be particularly relevant to learning support staff, cover supervisors, midday supervisors and after school supervisors.

Unit 2.1 Explore and respond to the needs of pupils

2.1.1 Explore how pupils develop their ability to think and learn

What you need to know and understand	*Refer to:*
(i) What the main stages of development of thinking and learning are in the pupils you work with	59–62
(ii) What factors can support and get in the way of the development of thinking and learning	57–65, 120–23
(iii) How to interact with pupils in ways that help to develop their ability to think and learn	57–65
(iv) How to listen, question, understand and respond to pupils and adults	40, 57, 74, 77–8
(v) What barriers to communication there may be (for example, where English is an additional language, disability or making hurried guesses about what people mean without checking)	44, 74, 77–8

2.1.2 Contribute to the well-being and safeguarding pupils

	What you need to know and understand	*Refer to:*
(i)	How to establish respectful, professional relationships with children, young people and adults	44, 57, 74, 77–8
(ii)	How to behave appropriately for a child or young person's stage of development	57–65
(iii)	How to reflect the values of the school in your day-to-day work	73–4, 79–80
(iv)	The importance of adults acting as good role models for pupils	43–4
(v)	What signs that children or young people may give that they are in danger of risk or harm	126, 128–9
(vi)	How to recognise signs of potential harm	126, 128–9
(vii)	The importance of sharing information when pupil's safety and wellbeing are concerned, maintaining confidentiality about sensitive information, except where the safety or welfare of the pupil means that it is appropriate to share with other people and agencies, respecting the confidences of pupils, except where it is overridden by the need to protect their safety	16, 33, 126, 128–9, 142–3, 149, 162, 196–7
(viii)	How to report, record and pass on information about pupils' safety and well-being	16–17, 118, 126, 142, 149, 165
(ix)	What the limits of your role and responsibilities are in supporting the pupils you work with and how to act on any remaining concerns you may have	16, 33, 142–3, 126, 128–9, 162, 196–7
(x)	When to involve others and where to get advice and support	126, 142, 161–2

Unit 2.2 Explore school values, policies, roles and responsibilities

2.2.1 Work within your school's values, policies and procedures

What you need to know and understand	*Refer to:*
(i) What the schools aims and values are	73–4
(ii) What laws affect work in school's, such as the Data Protection Act (1988); the UN Convention on Rights of the Child (1989); the Children Act (2004); equalities laws; the Freedom of Information Act (2000); and the Human Rights Act (1988)	19–20, 188–99
(iii) What the school's policies and procedures are, for example (equal opportunities; health and safety; confidentiality; data protection, use of language; behaviour management, discrimination; inclusion; disabilities; and diversity	4, 15, 19, 37–9, 72, 115, 130, 138–9, 142, 162, 165, 179
(iv) How to reflect the values of the school in your conduct	79–80

2.2.2 Explore the roles and responsibilities of teachers and others who work with pupils

What you need to know and understand	*Refer to:*
(i) The roles and responsibilities of teachers and others who work with pupils (for example, Head Teacher, other members of the senior management team, subject leaders and other posts such as special needs coordinator or First Aider)	11, 52–3, 75–6, 145
(ii) The roles and responsibilities of other support staff	11, 17–19, 36, 52–3, 75–6
(iii) Who the key post holders are	75–6
(iv) How your support role relates to the role of teachers, others who work with pupils and other support staff (for example, your line manager, colleagues and any other people you have contact with)	36, 73–6
(v) How to establish respectful, professional relationships with pupils and adults	44, 57, 74, 77–8
(vi) How to communicate effectively with pupils, staff and other adults	44, 57, 74, 77–8

2.2.3 Understand and develop your effectiveness in a support role

What you need to know and understand	*Refer to:*
(i) The limits of your role	36, 73–4, 149, 162
(ii) When to refer issues or people on	75–6, 126
(iii) How to get help and support when you are not sure about what to do	126, 149, 162
(iv) What areas of work you are effective in and any areas where you could improve	82–5
(v) How to respond positively to feedback from others about your work	74, 77–8
(vi) How to produce an action plan	89
(vii) What actions you could take to improve your skills, knowledge and effectiveness at work	82–5, 89

Bibliography

Aronson, E. and Patnoe, S. (1997) *The Jigsaw Classroom: Building Cooperation in the Classroom*, 2nd edn. New York: Addison Wesley Longman.

Berndt, T. J. (1983) Social cognition, social behaviour, and children's friendships. In E. T. Higgins, D. N. Ruble and W. W. Hartup (eds) *Social Cognition and Social Development: A Sociocultural Perspective*. Cambridge: Cambridge University Press.

City & Guilds (2003) *Level 2 NVQ for Teaching Assistants*. London: City & Guilds Publications, www.city-and-guilds.co.uk

Coie, J. D., Dodge, K. A. and Coppotelli, H. (1982) Dimensions and types of social status: A cross-age perspective. *Developmental Psychology*, 18: 557–570.

Damon, W. (1983) The nature of social-cognitive change in the developing child. In W. F. Overton (ed.) *The Relationship between Social and Cognitive Development*. Hillsdale, NJ: Erlbaum.

Daniels, H., Visser, J., Cole, T. and Reybekill, N. de (1999) *Emotional and Behavioural Difficulties in Mainstream Schools*, School of Education, University of Birmingham. London: HMSO.

Department for Education (DfE) (1994) *Code of Practice on the Identification and Assessment of Special Educational Needs*. London: HMSO.

Department for Education and Employment (DfEE) (1997) *Excellence for All Children: Meeting Special Educational Needs*. London: HMSO.

—— (1998) *A Programme for Action: Meeting Special Educational Needs*. London: HMSO.

—— (1999) *Social Inclusion: Pupil Support*. Circular 10/99. London: HMSO.

—— (2000) *Working with Teaching Assistants: A Good Practice Guide*. London: DfEE Publications.

—— (2001) *Special Educational Needs Code of Practice*. London: HMSO.

Department for Education and Science (DES) (1978) *Special Educational Needs: Report of the Committee of Enquiry into the Education of Handicapped Children and Young People (The Warnock Report)*. London: HMSO.

Department for Education and Skills (DfES) (2004a) *Every Child Matters: Change for Children*. Nottingham: DfES Publications, www.everychildmatters.gov.uk

—— (2004b) *Removing Barriers to Achievement: The Government's Strategy for SEN*. Nottingham: DfES Publications.

Erikson, E. H. (1982) *The Life Cycle Completed: A Review*. New York: Norton.

Gardner, H. (1993) *Frames of Mind*. New York: Basic Books.

Local Government National Training Organisation (LGNTO) (2001) *Teaching/Classroom Assistants Standards*, www.ukstandards.org

Lorenz, S. (2002) *First Steps in Inclusion*. London: David Fulton.

National Joint Council for Local Government Services (2003) *School Support Staff – The Way Forward*. London: The Employers' Organisation, www.lge.gov.uk

National Remodelling Team (2003) *Raising Standards and Tackling Workload: A National Agreement*, www.remodelling.org

Numicon, Unit D, Prospect House, The Hyde Business Park, Brighton, BN2 4JE.

OCR (2006) Support work in School Level 2 Award and Certificate www.ocr.org.uk

Piaget, J. (1970) *The Science of Education and the Psychology of the Child*. New York: Viking Press.

Qualifications and Curriculum Authority/Department for Education and Employment (QCA/DfEE) (2000) *The National Curriculum (Curriculum 2000) Inclusion Statement*. London: HMSO.

—— (2001) *Supporting the Target Setting Process*. London: HMSO.

Selman, R. L. (1980) *The Growth of Interpersonal Understanding*. New York: Academic Press.

Sigelman, C. K. and Shaffer, D. F. (1991) *Life-Span Human Development*. Belmont, CA: Brooks/Cole.

Training Development Agency (TDA) (2006) *Developing People to Support Learning: A Skills Strategy for the Wider School Workforce 2006–2009*, www.tda.gov.uk

United Nations Educational, Scientific and Cultural Organization (UNESCO) (1994) *The Salamanca Statement*. UNESCO.

Vygotsky, L. S. (1986) *Thought and Language*, new edn, ed. A. Kozulin. Cambridge, MA: MIT Press.

Index